Samba:
UNIX and NT Networking

James DeRoest

McGraw-Hill

New York   San Francisco   Washington, D.C.
Auckland   Bogotá   Caracas   Lisbon   London
Madrid   Mexico City   Milan   Montreal   New Delhi
San Juan   Singapore   Sydney   Tokyo   Toronto

McGraw-Hill

A Division of The McGraw·Hill Companies

Copyright © 2000 by the McGraw-Hill Companies. All rights reserved. Printed in the United States of America. Except as permitted under the United States Copyright Act of 1976, no part of this publication may be reproduced or distributed in any form or by any means, or stored in a data base or retrieval system, without the prior written permission of the publisher.

1 2 3 4 5 6 7 8 9 0   AGM/AGM   9 0 4 3 2 1 0 9

PN: 135105-1
Part of 0-07-135104-3

The sponsoring editor for this book was Simon Yates and the production supervisor was Clare Stanley. It was set in Janson Text by Patricia Wallenburg.

Printed and bound by Quebecor Martinsburg.

Throughout this book, trademarked names are used. Rather than put a trademark symbol after every occurrence of a trademarked name, we use names in an editorial fashion only, and to the benefit of the trademark owner, with no intention of infringement of the trademark. Where such designations appear in this book, they have been printed with initial caps.

 This book is printed on recycled, acid-free paper containing a minimum of 50% recycled, de-inked fiber.

*"I don't wish to be everything to everyone,
but I would like to be something to someone."*
Javan

To my Mother and Grandmothers,
Great and Grand.

Contents

Part 03   Configuration   97

Preface

Samba: UNIX and Windows Internetworking is a text describing how *Samba* can be used to unify and integrate network based file and print resources in a heterogeneous desktop and server computing environment. Along with a general discussion of how to install, configure and manage Samba, the text will also address how Samba can be used to resolve mobile computing synchronization problems, integrate authentication and access controls in small to large enterprises and interoperate with Windows 2000.

What Is Samba?

Samba is an Open Source software suite of UNIX services that enable MS Windows and other desktop clients to access UNIX file systems and printers via Microsoft's Server Message Block (SMB) and Common Internet File System (CIFS) protocols. Since its inception in 1991, Samba has continued to evolve and incorporate new features. The latest versions of Samba offer much of the functionality provided by the Windows NT Domain system. Originally used primarily within academia and research institutions, Samba has grown in popularity and is now supported by over 100 commercial vendors worldwide. Samba is readily available, including source code, for most UNIX platforms under the GNU General Public Licensing agreement. A sampling of supported clients include DOS, Windows for Workgroups 3.11, Windows 95/98, Windows NT OS/2, Macintosh, VMS, and MVS.

Audience

The target audience for this work includes systems programmers and administrators who are looking for assistance in implementing Samba in new and existing Windows and UNIX environments. A basic overview of both UNIX and Windows system and network architectures is provided to assist those readers whose primary background may be in one or the other of these operating environments. The general narrative of the text focuses on how to install and configure Samba to facilitate various authentication models favoring either UNIX or Windows as a primary security authority. This includes how Samba can be configured to act as an NT Primary Domain Controller and how Samba coexists with Windows 2000. The subject matter is partitioned by function to facilitate quick access to topics of interest. Advanced topics are integrated into each of the functional chapters to reduce having to move back and forth between general and advanced chapters. Sections on operation and client tools will benefit end users who want a better understanding of how to tailor and optimize their use of Samba services.

Chapter Tour

Chapter 1 begins with an overview of the problems and challenges of internetworking computing resources in a mixed UNIX and Windows environment. Trouble spots include maintaining application preference consistency for mobile users, resource scaling and naming in large enterprises, and password synchronization between dissimilar operating systems. The intent is to assist the reader in identifying their own requirements for planning an infrastructure to facilitate resource sharing under Samba.

Chapter 2 is for those administrators and users who are unfamiliar with the UNIX operating system and its network services. Since Samba runs as a UNIX based service, the focus of discussion centers on those UNIX subsystems important to the care and feeding of Samba. The chapter also includes an overview of the various UNIX naming, authentication, and authorization services referenced in later chapters regarding resource identification and access control.

Chapter 3 is similar to Chapter 2 in that it presents an overview of the various Windows implementations and architectures. Special attention is devoted to the NETBIOS, SMB, and CIFS protocols upon which Samba is based. Other topics include name service, authentication and access controls, browsing, and Windows 2000 Active Directory.

Chapter 4 introduces Samba, its history, and its evolution. The chapter follows from the previous discussions of UNIX and Windows architectures by outlining how Samba facilitates authentication, authorization, and resource sharing between the two operating systems. The chapter also covers licensing and distribution, and concludes with a brief overview of Samba NT Primary Domain Controller emulation.

Chapter 5 provides further detail on the Samba distribution package, supported platforms, documentation, and the installation process. Installation trade offs related to the binary and source distribution formats are presented, along with a step by step procedure for building Samba from source code. The chapter closes with an introduction to Samba configuration, system startup, and operation.

Chapter 6 begins the advanced section of the text by further detailing Samba configuration options. This chapter is intended to be a base reference of stanzas, variables, and parameters which will be used in configuring the services presented in subsequent chapters. This section also includes a discussion of the use of Samba macros which can be used to automate administration and operation tasks.

Chapter 7 focuses on authentication and access control mechanisms. Alternative schemes for mapping accounts, groups, and permissions are presented along with techniques for integrating Samba with the more advanced authentication mechanisms provided by NDIS, Kerberos, LDAP, and Windows 2000. The chapter also covers password security and name space scaling for large enterprises.

Chapter 8 describes the various name service mechanisms supported by Samba to identify and locate resources in a domain or workgroup. Approaches include the use of host files, names servers like WINS and DNS, and interoperating with Windows 2000 Active Directory.

Chapter 9 follows the previous discussion on resource identification with a description of how to setup the browse service to manage resource visibility by Windows clients in the network. Topics include the use of browse lists, the browser election process, and browsing over local and routed subnets.

Chapter 10 explains how to configure Samba to emulate an NT Primary Domain Controller (PDC). The discussion covers the features and limitations in the PDC implementation, defining trust relationships with other domains, setting up user profiles, policies and login scripts, and interoperability issues with Windows 2000 domains, trees, and forests.

Chapter 11 describes how files and directories are shared between UNIX and Windows via Samba. The chapter presents a number of problem areas that must be considered when configuring Samba file shares. Areas requiring special consideration include mapping file name structures and character sets, support for symbolic links, and file locking mechanisms.

Chapter 12 covers the configuration of printer shares in Samba. The discussion covers configuration for various styles of UNIX printing, driver support, and queuing controls. This section also describes printing from UNIX to Windows managed printers.

Chapter 13 switches focus from the server side of Samba to its various clients. Step by step instructions are provided for configuring Windows, UNIX, and other desktop clients to authenticate and the access the resources managed by Samba.

Chapter 14 outlines administrative tasks and tools which will help the reader maintain a reliable and available Samba service. This includes descriptions of graphical and Web-based tools which simplify Samba administration.

Chapter 15 culminates the text with on overview of troubleshooting procedures for diagnosing and correcting problems. A synopsis of the tools available in Samba, UNIX, and Windows is provided along with descriptions of how they can be used together to sleuth Samba problems. A listing of additional Samba documents and on-line discussion groups is provided for those "when all else fails—cry for help" situations.

The appendices provide example configurations and additional reference information.

That being said, it's time to *Samba*!

Part 01

Introduction and Planning

Internetworking UNIX and Windows

When network engineers talk about *internetworking*, the flow of conversation usually eddies around the various lower-level protocols and circuits involved in the connectivity between some set of networked devices, be it computers, routers, switches, or just about any pair of semi-intelligent appliances. They don't normally use the term when discussing connectivity between services residing higher up in the protocol stack (Table 1.1).

Anything above layer 3 or 4 is just a glob or cloud that represents the endpoints in a networked conversation. System administrators, on the other hand, tend to extend the scope of internetworking to include the union of protocols and upper-layer services that result in some meaningful unit of interoperation between the cooperating systems. An example is the set protocols and services required to share files between platform "A" and platform "B". Given that a common set of supported protocols can be found, it is generally possible to build the corresponding set of software services to facilitate resource sharing even between quite dissimilar operating systems. Enter "Samba," which represents just such a suite of software services working in concert with standard protocols like *Server Message Block (SMB)*, *Common Internet File System (CIFS)*, *NetBIOS*, and *Transmission Control Protocol (TCP)* to internetwork UNIX and Windows-based resources (Figure 1.1). Thus the title for this text: *Samba: UNIX and Windows Internetworking*.

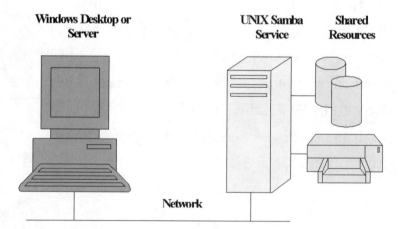

Figure 1.1   *UNIX, Windows, and Samba*

Table 1.1 *OSI Protocol Stack*

Layer	Description
7 Application	User interface and services
6 Presentation	Application data transformations
5 Session	Connection authentication
4 Transport	End-to-end data ordering
3 Network	Routing and reporting mechanisms
2 Data	Packet format, integrity, and address
1 Physical	Physical hardware specification

Why do we speak of UNIX and MS Windows internetworking? It is not uncommon these days to find a growing mixture of UNIX and Windows-based systems coexisting, for better or worse, in most organizations. This might seem a bit odd given that these operating systems are incarnations of somewhat different development histories and philosophies (Tables 1.2 and 1.3). One is driven from an open systems and standards perspective and the other represents a more proprietary attitude, with a focus on business and personal use requirements. This is not to say that over time each of these operating systems has not had to address all of these issues to compete in the marketplace. Each has its own strengths and weaknesses. This is likely why we are seeing a marriage of these platforms within most enterprises today. One complements the other in addressing the demands of the complex heterogeneous computing environments found in businesses, schools, and even the home.

The importance of seamlessly internetworking these two worlds has gained the attention of traditional "UNIX-only" user groups like the USENIX Association. Over the last few years USENIX has held special symposia dedicated to UNIX and Windows NT integration. The USENIX *Large Installation Systems Administration (LISA)* group has also held conferences on UNIX and Windows topics. In most instances attendance at these conferences has been close to overbooked.

Table 1.2 *UNIX Development History*

1969 – Thompson develops single-user system on DEC PDP-7

1970 – Kernighan coins the name UNIX

1973 – Ritchie develops C language
UNIX rewritten in C

1974 – ACM publishes Thompson and Ritchie's paper on UNIX

1975 – Bell Labs licenses UNIX V6 to universities

1977 – SCO and Interactive Systems founded
Thompson & Joy develop BSD 1.0

1978 – UNIX Version 7
BSD 2.0

1979 – Berkeley ARPAnet Contract
BSD 3.0

1980 – BSD 4.0
Microsoft develops XENIX

1981 – SUN founded

1982 – AT&T System III
SUN becomes Sun Microsystems

1983 – AT&T System V
BSD 4.2
SUN SunOS
Hewlett-Packard HP-UX
GNU Project conceived

1984 – AT&T System V.2
DEC ULTRIX
X/Open Founded

1985 – Sun NFS
POSIX 1003.1 published

1986 – AT&T SYSV.3, Streams, RFS
BSD 4.3
IBM AIX RT
Commercial X Windows release

1987 – AT&T SYSV.3.1

1988 – AT&T SYSV.3.2
BSD 4.3 Tahoe

1989 – AT&T SYSV.4
Open Software Foundation Founded
OSF Motif
UNIX International Founded
Internet Worm on Nov 2

continued on next page

Table 1.2   *continued*

1990 –	BSD 4.3Reno
	IBM AIX RS/6000
	OSF/1
1991 –	Apple, IBM, Motorola Venture
	Sun Solaris 1.0
	Linux 0.02
1992 –	BSD 4.4
1993 –	Novell buys UNIX System Laboratories
	Novell grants UNIX trademark to X/Open
	386BSD 1.0
	FreeBSD 1.0
	NetBSD 0.8
1994 –	Linux 1.0
	Linux International
1998 –	Open Source Program

UNIX has been around for about 30 years. Initially found primarily in academia and research environments, it is a powerful multiuser, multitasking operating system suitable for a wide range of applications. It is easily scalable from small single-user workstations to very large mainframe, multiprocessor, and cluster computing architectures supporting thousands of simultaneous users and processes. Because of the availability of source code, built-in programming environment, and a solid focus on standard interfaces and protocols, UNIX is easily ported to most hardware platforms. This has resulted in a rich set of public and vendor implementations. Yet general access to source code has also kept UNIX somewhat vendor independent. When we use the term "UNIX" we are usually referring to the full array of public and vendor versions available in the marketplace. It is true that each rendition of UNIX tends to have its own nuances, add-on features, and variations on the basic theme, but in general functionality has remained quite consistent across platforms over its long development history. In fact, the collective expertise of this large development community has greatly contributed to the overall maturity, interoperability, and robustness of the operating system.

On the down side, the most prominent complaint concerning UNIX is directed at its character-based command-line user interface. Although the rich set of commands, interpretive shells, and scripting languages provide a great deal of functionality for the programmer and systems administrator, their use and existence are not easy for the novice user. Most commands are cryptic shorthand strings and often derive context from the shell under which they are invoked. This can be quite confusing to all but experienced users. A graphical user interface called X Windows can be added to the operating system, but it does not entirely shield the user from the intricacies of the command interface. Another criticism is that although most applications can be easily ported between the various versions of UNIX, they are generally not binary-compatible from one vendor platform to another. This has tended to limit the availability of some products across all UNIX platforms.

UNIX has found a home in many businesses because of its open interfaces and tight integration with Internet technologies. UNIX and the Internet grew up together. As specifications for internetworking protocols like TCP/IP were developed, they were quickly interwoven into the networking fabric of UNIX. Most of what we have come to expect concerning basic information-sharing services over the Internet were developed under UNIX. This has enabled UNIX to be used as a protocol and server Swiss Army knife for quickly and cost effectively connecting legacy proprietary computing infrastructures to the Internet.

Table 1.3   *Windows Development History*

1980 –   IBM contracts with Microsoft for PC OS
         Bill Gates buys QDOS
         MS-DOS created from QDOS

1981 –   First IBM PC
         MS begins "Interface Manager" development

1983 –   Windows announced
         MS-DOS 2.0

1985 –   Windows 1.0
         Dropdown menus
         Mouse support

1987 –   Windows 2.0
         Icons and overlapping windows
         MS & IBM begin work on OS/2

continued on next page

Table 1.3 *continued*

	MS & IBM split on OS/2 and Windows development
	Windows/386
1990 –	Windows 3.0
	Program and File Manager
	Network support
1991 –	Windows 3.1
	Object Linking and Embedding (OLE)
	Multimedia
	MS begins work on "New Technology" OS
1994 –	Windows NT 3.1 32-bit OS
	Protected mode
	Security
	Windows for Workgroups 3.11
	Win32s
1995 –	Windows 95
	Pre-emptive multitasking
	Threads
1996 –	Windows NT 4.0
	Windows CE
	IBM ends OS/2 development
1997 –	Windows 95 OSR2
	Active Desktop
	FAT32
	Includes Internet Explorer 3.0
1998–	Windows 98
	Integrated Internet Explorer 4.0
1999 –	Windows 98 SE
	Internet Explorer 5.0
	Windows NT 5.0 renamed Windows 2000
	Windows 2000 Beta3 Release Candidate1

The Microsoft Windows success story can be easily attributed to its point-and-click user interface and low-cost hardware platform. The widespread familiarity with the Windows interface, its rich set of productivity tools, and its commodity hardware component base have quickly made it the predominant world standard in single user desktop computing. This is pretty impressive feat considering it is little more than half the age of UNIX. Microsoft has done a very good job of embracing networking technologies, incorporating standards, and enhancing the user interface to extend productivity from the desktop to the workgroup and most recently the Internet. This began with peer-to-peer networking in Windows for Workgroups. Next came interoperability with Novell-based networks, client/server networking with Windows NT and UNIX, and strong Internet connectivity with tools such as Internet Explorer.

On the server side, the Microsoft story is still relatively new. *Windows NT (New Technology)* is only a little over five years old, yet in this short time it has captured a significant portion of the database client/server market. Windows NT incorporated bits and pieces of UNIX, VMS, OS/2, Netware, and existing Windows architectures to provide a multitasking networking service designed for tighter integration of and administer workgroup LANs under a new structure called *domains*. NT version 4.0 provided Windows-based networks closer ties with the Internet by including common Internet services like DNS, FTP, web, and SMTP-based electronic mail. Windows 2000 will extend this functionality by including additional internetworking tools like LDAP directory services, Kerberos authentication, and public-key services, each of which is closely linked to existing Windows networking and security services.

Although touted as the UNIX-killer, Windows NT has yet to fully replace UNIX services in the back room. Likewise UNIX does not provide the tight desktop support services and friendly user and administration interfaces that have been the hallmark of Windows. The result is that both operating systems are common fixtures in most shops. The challenge, then, for the system administrator is how best to simplify the administrative and management tasks of maintaining both operating systems, and how to facilitate seamless user access to the resources that reside in each world. This is where services like Samba become essential tools to smoothing the rough edges of UNIX's and Windows' coexistence.

Planning

Before we jump into the nuts and bolts of Samba installation and configuration, we need to look carefully at the existing infrastructure, identify the problem areas and inconsistencies to be resolved, and develop an architecture that will allow incorporation of new technologies such as Windows 2000. Most architecture upgrades are not complete replacements for existing systems, so we need an implementation strategy that permits coexistence of older services alongside new development. Begin by asking questions like:

- Is the existing OS base primarily UNIX or Windows?
- Are in-house systems administration skills predominantly UNIX or Windows?
- What resources need to be accessible in both OS worlds?
- Is the focus for resource sharing directed at desktops, servers, or both?
- What desktop clients need to be supported?
- Is user mobility an issue?
- Will there be an impact on existing business models?
- Is scaling an issue concerning number of users, desktops, and/or servers?
- What level of availability is required?
- Will resource sharing require changes in namespace?
- Is it necessary to synchronize accounts and passwords?
- What level of access controls is required?
- Is the setup domain, workgroup- or realm-based?
- Will network topology affect browsing and access control?

These are only a few of the issues that will require scrutiny before adding Samba to an environment. Since there are underlying complexities to each of these, we'll look closer at a few of them in the next sections of this chapter.

Desktop Issues

Almost everyone has a computer these days. Most of us have access to more than one: palmtop, handheld, laptop, home PC, office workstation, and network server, the list goes on and on. We spend much of our time computer hopping from one network island to the next. The boundaries between the machines, networks, and services we use have blurred to the point where it is difficult to pinpoint where particular resources reside. We find ourselves wondering if we left that memo on the office workstation or on the PC in the den at home?

The challenge then for the system administrator is in providing an environment which assists mobile computer users in maintaining consistent access to documents, mail folders, address books, web certificates, bookmarks, and other application-preference data as they move from machine to machine. The task of synchronizing state is complicated by variations in data formats and network protocols when the set of machines includes both UNIX and Windows operating systems.

A twist on the problem of maintaining individual state between multiple computers is how to manage state on a single computer used by multiple people. Consider the public computers in airports, libraries, university labs, and cyber cafes. What level of environment personalization should be allowed, if any? How will environment state be maintained and reset after each use to ensure both privacy and security? If personal environment profiles are going to be maintained, what are the scaling issues regarding account management and storage?

Enterprise Computing Issues

The evolution of bringing legacy information services to the Internet community has seen most enterprises move away from proprietary, restricted access, and network computing architectures to more open distributed computing models. This has most often been facilitated by incorporating UNIX servers into the network to mitigate the information flow between data warehouse systems and the Internet. The result is increased operating system heterogeneity in the data center, which must be managed by systems administration and operations staff.

The addition of new operating systems usually includes additional complexity in maintaining a consistent namespace of users, machines and services. For example, differences in supported character sets require the formulation of intricate character mappings between the various systems. Large user populations may require duplicating and managing the user account and password spaces on each platform. Users may also be required to login and logout repeatedly as they access resources that reside on various systems.

Domains and Realms

In many organizations the authentication, authorization, and trust models built into the computing and networking infrastructure closely match those represented in organizational structure and processes. Trust between machines is as critical as trust between employees. A new operating system can often throw a kink into day-to-day operation when it does not fit within the existing structure. Transitive trust rules that follow organizational administrative roles usually work well between like operating systems as, for example, trust between UNIX Kerberos realms or trust between Windows NT domains. The same capability is not always as seamless when one is trying to map access control and group relationships between dissimilar architectures. Windows 2000 brings additional complexity into these trust mechanisms with its hybrid authentication and authorization framework. Incorporating Windows 2000 into existing NT domain topologies requires careful planning for how domain relationships will be migrated into the new domain tree and forest model. There are also a number of issues which must be resolved regarding two-way synchronization between Windows 2000 and UNIX Kerberos namespaces.

Passwords

An additional side effect of the mobility problem just described is that when one uses multiple computers, there tend to be multiple accounts and passwords corresponding to each platform. It can be a real challenge for users and administrators to attempt to keep accounts and passwords synchronized between diverse operating systems. There is also an additional security exposure in that encryption algorithms used on one system may not be supported on the other. The result may mean transmitting clear-text passwords over unsecured networks or maintaining password lists on unsecured workstations.

Sharing Resources with Samba

Most of the issues described above can be resolved through the use of mutually supported software tools like Sun's *Network File System*

(NFS) or *Novell Netware*, which provide a means for sharing files, printers and access controls between UNIX and Windows. A robust and cost-effective alternative is Samba, developed by Andrew Tridgell. Samba is a drop-in replacement for the file- and print-sharing services normally provided by Windows NT- or LAN Manager-based systems. Samba augments these services by also encompassing UNIX file systems and printers in the mix of shared resources. Other Samba services include NetBIOS name service for browsing and limited NT Primary Domain Controller emulation. Since its inception in 1991 Samba has grown in popularity; it is now supported by over 100 commercial vendors worldwide. It has been ported to most flavors of UNIX as well as proprietary operating systems like VMS and MVS.

In the next two chapters we will review the protocols and system services in UNIX and Windows that are critical to understanding and maintaining Samba. These chapters will benefit those system administrators and programmers who may be unfamiliar with one or the other of these operating systems. The remainder of the text will focus on Samba architecture, installation, configuration, and support tasks.

UNIX Overview

In the '60s the adage was never to trust anyone over 30. UNIX is quickly approaching the age of 30-something, but contrary to this adage, I believe we can continue to rely on UNIX's consistent, open and portable computing architecture well into its next decade. Over the years UNIX has evolved into a robust cross-platform, multi-tasking, multi-processing, multi-user operating system complete with a rich application and programming base. In this chapter we will focus on the UNIX tools and services required to support Samba. We will also cover general networking concepts important in internetworking UNIX and Windows resources. Those readers who have already earned their UNIX wizard's merit badge may want to skip this chapter and go right to the next chapter, on Windows.

Architecturally, UNIX can best be visualized as a tiered set of services and interfaces (Figure 2.1). At the foundation of the structure resides the *kernel*, which is responsible for managing the interfaces between all hardware components and the execution environment. This includes scheduling work, allocating memory, moving data, and informing tasks when various system events occur. On top of the kernel layer resides the *shell*. The shell, of which there is more than one, is essentially a command interpreter that accepts input, provides context, and requests services of the kernel on behalf of the user. The penthouse level of the UNIX tier comprises the user interface. Here reside all the commands, scripting languages, graphical interfaces, and utilities that enable the end-user to interoperate with the resources provided by the operating system. An important concept to remember when working with UNIX is that the general interface between all the system objects is that every object is abstracted as a file. This means that all operations are file operations regardless of whether the target is hardware, data, memory, or running tasks.

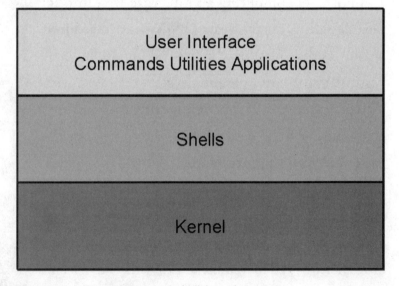

Figure 2.1   *UNIX Command, shell, kernel structure*

Services and Daemons

Each running task, along with its associated address space, is called a *process*. The group of active processes running under UNIX is analogous to the generations of a family tree. *Child* processes are begotten by *parent* processes. Processes are born, live out their lives, and then pass away. Occasionally they may even run away. The first process to run on every UNIX system is called `init`. `Init` is the great-grandparent from which all process generations owe their existence. Like any loving grandparent, `init` even takes in orphan processes that have lost their immediate parents. During the course of its life, each process wants to take a turn on the CPU. Just like children, processes the guidance of a scheduler to ensure that every process receives its fair share of CPU time. The system administrator acts as the grand overseer of the process universe, wielding ultimate control over the lives of all processes.

Every process in the UNIX universe is christened with a positive integer number called the *Process Identifier (PID)*. The PID is a vector index in the process table maintained by the kernel. PIDs are unique and are allocated in a somewhat random fashion. Process table entries point to per-process kernel data structures which define the attributes and values associated with the given process (Table 2.1). The attributes of active processes can be interrogated from the command line by using the `ps` command (Example 2.1).

Table 2.1   *Sampling of Process Attributes*

Process Identifier

Process Group Identifier

Process Parent Identifier

Process Owner

Effective and Real User and Group Identifiers

Priority

Controlling Terminal

Address Space

Size in Pages

Paging Statistics

Resource Utilization

Process State

Example 2.1   *Displaying Process Attributes*

```
# ps -elk                   SYSV Process Display Format
F     S    UID PID PPID C   PRI NI  ADDR  SZ    WCHAN TTY TIME CMD
303   A    0   0   0    120 16  707 4     -     0:05 swapper
200003 A   0   1   0    0   60  20  505   220   -     0:07 init
40401 A    0   8626 1   0   60  20  69fa  1060  -     0:09 nmbd
40001 A    0   8664 1   0   60  20  49f2  1440  -     0:06 smbd


# ps auxw                   BSD Process Display Format
USER  PID  %CPU %MEM SZ   RSS  TTY  STAT STIME     TIME COMMAND
root  1    0.1  0.0  220  180  -    A    00:19:58  0:07 /etc/init
root  0    0.1  0.0  4    8    -    A    00:19:28  0:05 swapper
root  8626 0.0  1.0  1060 852  -    A    00:20:17  0:09 nmbd -D -f nmbd.pid
root  8664 0.0  1.0  1440 808  -    A    00:20:41  0:06 smbd -D -f smbd.pid
```

It will be helpful to understand a few of the columns displayed in the list of running processes when managing execution resources in a running system. The COMMAND and CMD columns represent the program being run in the process address space. Along with its PID, each process records the integer ID of its *Parent Process Identifier (PPID)*. Process short-term CPU usage, execution priority, and nice value are displayed in the PRI, C, and NI fields in the SYSV display. The BSD #CPU field represents the percentage of CPU resources that a process has used in its life time.

In every process universe there is a special set of processes called *daemons*. A daemon is not some miscreant process spawned by some evil hacker to wreck havoc on a system, but a collection of one or more processes that provide some well-defined service. For example, the sendmail daemon manages and distributes electronic mail on behalf of the UNIX user community. In the case of Samba, the smbd daemon manages access to shared resources. The Samba nmbd daemon provides name service to assist clients in locating resource shares.

Init

I've already mentioned the special role that init plays as the ancestor of all processes on the running system. Init is responsible for *spawning* some of the important system daemons at system startup and "respawning" processes that may have exited due to some unforeseen event. These processes are identified in a configuration file called /etc/inittab. Entries in the inittab configuration file take the form:

```
<identifier>:<runlevel>:<action>:<command>
```

The *identifier* field uniquely identifies the service. The *runlevel* corresponds to the running system state which will cause the *action* to be invoked on the *command*. Runlevels are represented as numbers 0 through 9 and indicate various system states. An example inittab entry for the cron daemon which time schedules batch jobs on UNIX would look like:

```
cron:2:respawn:/usr/sbin/cron        Inittab cron process entry
```

As we shall see in a following section, there are other mechanisms available for spawning service daemons. In the case of network-based services like Samba, it is often desirable to initiate an instance of a service daemon only at the actual time when its services are requested by a client.

Networking

Understanding UNIX TCP/IP network configuration and administration is important in this context because it is used as the transport for Samba NetBIOS services. *NetBIOS over TCP/IP (NetBT)* is defined in RFCs 1001 and 1002. We will take a closer look at NetBT in the Windows networking section of the following chapter.

TCP/IP

When we talk about TCP/IP we are referring to a larger set of protocols that comprise the general functionality associated with service (Table 2.2). In the TCP/IP stack model, these protocols are bundled into a smaller number of layers than defined in the OSI model.

Table 2.2   *Common Lower-Layer Internet Protocols*

IP	Internet Protocol
ICMP	Internet Control Message Protocol
ARP	Address Resolution Protocol
RARP	Reverse Address Resolution Protocol
TCP	Transmission Control Protocol
UDP	User Datagram Protocol

			NFS	
Application OSI 5–7	TELNET, SMTP, FTP, ETC	TFTP, SNMP, ETC	RPC	
Transport OSI 4	TCP	UDP		
Internetwork OSI 3	IP	ICMP	ARP	RARP
Physical OSI 1–2	Ethernet, Token Ring, FDDI, SOCC, HiPPI, ETC			

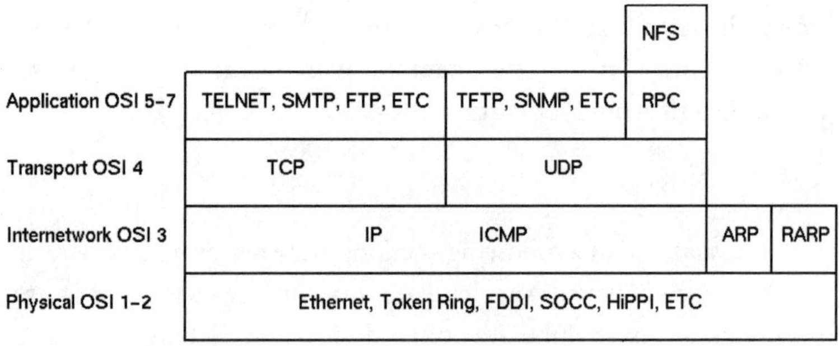

Figure 2.2   *TCP/IP and OSI stack*

The *Physical* layer represents a conglomeration of hardware interfaces and protocols that interoperate via the conduit defined in the upper layers. These interfaces employ a wide range of data speeds and physical architectures.

The *Internetwork* layer combines the OSI data-link layer and a portion of the OSI network layer. The layer is comprised of two protocols, Internet Protocol (IP) and Internet Control Message Protocol (ICMP). IP and ICMP are connectionless protocols that provide the basic data buckets and control in the network.

The *Transport* layer defines two protocols, Transmission Control Protocol (TCP) and User Datagram Protocol (UDP). TCP ensures a reliable ordered transport whereas UDP service is unreliable and does not ensure delivery.

The *Application* layer in the TCP/IP suite, like the OSI model, implements the user interface. Client/server protocols are most often defined at the application layer.

Addressing

A unique IP address is assigned by the network administrator to represent each computer in the network. The IP address abstracts the hardware address to a more general use. At this address level we are not concerned with the adapter interface type used on a particular machine. Each IP address is a 32-bit number represented as four octets. Each octet is a number in the range of 0 through 255:

```
<0-255>.<0-255>.<0-255>.<0-255>
```

In large networks, it is often desirable to group and partition computers to localize traffic patterns, hide internal network structure, simplify information routing, and enforce security policy. This is done using a system called *subnets*. A *subnet mask* is used to mask out a portion of the IP address to determine how traffic from the particular computer will be routed to other computers in the network. When a machine within the organization wants to send a packet to another system, it applies the subnet mask to the destination address to see if the address is on the local network or if it must send it to a router for delivery.

The subnet mask is a four-octet number that indicates which bits in the address are to be masked as the network and subnet portion of the address. The low-order bits of the mask designate the host portion of the address.

```
netmask 0xfffffff0 14 hosts per subnet (0 and 15 excluded)
netmask 0xfffffff8  6 hosts per subnet (0 and 7 excluded)
```

Understanding the subnet structure of the network will be important when you begin defining resources to be shared between systems which may exist on different subnets.

Domain Name Service

Although IP addresses uniquely identify computers and associated resources on the network, they are not easily remembered by human beings when trying to find those computers and resources. The simple solution to this kind of brain fault is to map easily remembered text strings to the associated IP numbers. A table of machine names and IP addresses can be installed on each computer to act as a directory of known systems. Under UNIX this directory of host name and IP number pairs is called the /etc/hosts table (Example 2.2).

Host tables work well for small networks but immediately break down as we scale up to large numbers of systems. Mapping host names to IP numbers for a large set of networks like the Internet is subject to the same scaling problems encountered when mapping personal and business names to phone numbers for all the cities in a particular country. There are far too many name collisions and the phone book is too large for timely incorporation and distribution of updates.

Example 2.2   */etc/hosts*

```
#
# IP Number          Host Names
#
127.0.0.1            localhost
128.95.135.13        daffy
128.95.135.24        louie
128.95.142.30        huey
140.27.133.4         donald
```

To address the scaling problem, a hierarchical namespace methodology was adopted for the Internet community which enforces uniqueness and supports timely distribution of updates. This namespace system is a client/server protocol called *BIND Domain Name Service (DNS)*.

Computers and organizations in DNS are identified by a *domain name*. The domain name is a string tuple delimited by "."s which represents the administrative hierarchy of the namespace (Table 2.3). Domain names are usually represented in two to four levels. Note that there is no implied mapping of domain names to IP number octets or subnets.

Table 2.3   *Domain Names*

Format:	hostname.subdomain.subdomain.topdomain
Examples:	microsoft.com
	vnet.ibm.com

A hierarchical name resolving protocol called *BIND* is used to recursively query *domain name servers* until a domain name is resolved to an IP number. In the DNS hierarchy (Figure 2.3), upper-level domain servers need only record the names of the next lower level of the name tuple along with the IP numbers of the name servers that resolve addresses for that level. All name servers must know the addresses of the top level Internet name servers which maintain a set of well-known top-level domain names (Table 2.4). The DNS system supports local management of the namespace and ensures timely information to the network at large.

Table 2.4   *Top Level Domains*

edu	Education
gov	Government
mil	Military
org	Organizations
com	Commercial
net	Other networks
Country Code	Two-character international identifier

On the server side, DNS is implemented under UNIX by the named daemon. Usually only a pair of DNS servers, primary and secondary, are configured for a given organization. It is not necessary to run named on each machine in a network. The named daemon obtains configuration information from the set of configuration files listed in Table 2.5. The full scope of the format and syntax of these tables is often complex and beyond the purpose of this text. The reader is directed to documentation regarding DNS setup and configuration for the given UNIX platform.

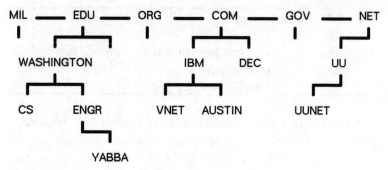

Figure 2.3   *Sample Internet domain hierarchy*

Table 2.5   *Named Configuration Files*

named.boot	Default domain, zone and authority
named.ca	Domain root cache prime information
named.data	Local domain information
named.rev	Reverse query information

All the machines in the organization which will be using DNS need to know where to find the primary and secondary name servers. This information is recorded in a `resolv.conf` file on each machine (Example 2.3). When a domain name is resolved to an IP address, a query is sent to the first name server in the `resolv.conf` list. If timeout period expires before an answer is received from the first name server, then the second name server is queried.

Example 2.3   *resolv.conf*

```
; /etc/resolv.conf
;
domain        foo.bar.org    ; default domain
nameserver    123.145.100.1  ; name server1
nameserver    123.145.100.2  ; name server2
```

Inetd

Instead of running some of the TCP/IP service daemons continuously, they can be started when a request is made for the service and stopped when the service has been completed. This capability is supported by the `inetd` daemon. Configuration information for inetd is located in the `/etc/inetd.conf` and `/etc/services` files (Examples 2.4 and 2.5). Entries in the `/etc/inetd.conf` file indicate each service name and any required startup information. The `/etc/service` file lists the service name, whether it uses TCP or UDP protocols, and the well-known port number associated with the service. Each time updates are made to either of these tables the `inetd` daemon must be refreshed. This can be done by sending a *hangup signal* to the `inetd` PID.

```
# kill -HUP <inetd-PID>
```

Example 2.4   */etc/inetd.conf*

```
# inted.conf
#
# service socket protocol wait/  user server  server program
# name    type           nowait      program      arguments
#
echo      stream   tcp nowait   root internal
echo      dgram    udp wait     root internal
discard   stream   tcp nowait   root internal
discard   dgram    udp wait     root internal
daytime   stream   tcp nowait   root internal
daytime   dgram    udp wait     root internal
chargen   stream   tcp nowait   root internal
chargen   dgram    udp wait     root internal
ftp       stream   tcp nowait   root /etc/ftpd ftpd
telnet    stream   tcp nowait   root /etc/telnetd telnetd
time      stream   tcp nowait   root internal
time      dgram    udp wait     root internal
bootps    dgram    udp wait     root /etc/bootpd bootpd
tftp      dgram    udp wait     nobody /etc/tftpd tftpd -n
finger    stream   tcp nowait   nobody /etc/fingerd fingerd
exec      stream   tcp nowait   root /etc/rexecd rexecd
login     stream   tcp nowait   root /etc/rlogind rlogind
shell     stream   tcp nowait   root /etc/rshd rshd
talk      dgram    udp wait     root /etc/talkd talkd
ntalk     dgram    udp wait     root /etc/talkd talkd
```

continued on next page

Example 2.4   *continued*

```
uucp           stream    tcp nowait  root /etc/uucpd uucpd
comsat         dgram     udp wait    root /etc/comsat comsat
netbios-ssn    stream    tcp nowait  root /usr/local/samba/bin/smbd
netbios-ns     dgram     udp wait    root /usr/local/samba/bin/nmbd
```

Example 2.5   */etc/services*

```
#
# Network well known services
#
# Service Port/Protocol Aliases
#
echo           7/tcp
echo           7/udp
discard        9/tcp     sink null
discard        9/udp     sink null
systat         11/tcp    users
daytime        13/tcp
daytime        13/udp
netstat        15/tcp
qotd           17/tcp    quote
chargen        19/tcp    ttytst source
chargen        19/udp    ttytst source
ftp-data       20/tcp
ftp            21/tcp
telnet         23/tcp
smtp           25/tcp    mail
time           37/tcp    timserver
time           37/udp    timserver
rlp            39/udp    resource      # resource location
nameserver     42/udp    name          # IEN 116
whois          43/tcp    nicname
domain         53/tcp    nameserver    # name-domain server
domain         53/udp    nameserver
mtp            57/tcp    # deprecated
bootps         67/udp    # bootp server port
bootpc         68/udp    # bootp client port
```

continued on next page

Example 2.5 *continued*

```
tftp          69/udp
rje           77/tcp   netrje
finger        79/tcp
link          87/tcp   ttylink
supdup        95/tcp
hostnames     101/tcp  hostname # usually from sri-nic
iso_tsap      102/tcp
x400          103/tcp
x400-snd      104/tcp
csnet-ns      105/tcp
pop           109/tcp  postoffice
sunrpc        111/tcp
sunrpc        111/udp
auth          113/tcp  authentication
sftp          115/tcp
uucp-path     117/tcp
nntp          119/tcp  readnews untp
ntp           123/tcp
ntp           123/udp           # network time protocol (exp)
netbios-udp   137/udp           # netbios udp
netbios-ssn   139/tcp           # netbios tcp
NeWS          144/tcp
snmp          161/udp           # snmp request port
snmp-trap     162/udp           # snmp monitor trap port
mux           199/tcp           # snmpd smux port
src           200/udp           # System Resource controller
exec          512/tcp
login         513/tcp
who           513/udp  whod
shell         514/tcp  cmd      # no passwords used
syslog        514/udp
printer       515/tcp  spooler  # line printer spooler
talk          517/udp
ntalk         518/udp
efs           520/tcp           # for LucasFilm
route         520/udp  router routed
timed         525/udp  timeserver
tempo         526/tcp  newdate
courier       530/tcp  rpc
conference    531/tcp  chat
netnews       532/tcp  readnews
```

continued on next page

Example 2.5   *continued*

```
netwall       533/udp            # for emergency broadcasts
uucp          540/tcp  uucpd     # uucp daemon
new-rwho      550/udp
remotefs      556/tcp  rfs_server rfs
rmonitor      560/udp
monitor       561/udp
```

File Systems

A UNIX file system is a partition of blocks on one or more disks that acts as a container for a directory and file tree. The primary structures which make up the file system are the *super block, inodes,* and *data blocks.*

The super block describes the overall structure of the file system. It contains the file system name, the size, pointer to the inode and free block lists, etc. The super block is used to keep track of the file system state during operation which may later be used to verify the integrity of the file system as part of the boot process and in the event of a failure.

Each directory and file in the file system is represented by an inode. The inode can be thought of as an index entry. Each inode is sequentially numbered from 1 up to the maximum number of inodes defined for the file system. The inode identifies the attributes of the file or directory it represents (Table 2.6).

Table 2.6   *Inode File Attributes*

File Mode
File Type
Owning UID and GID
Date and Time Stamps
Number of Links
Pointer to Data Blocks
Size in Bytes
Size in Blocks

Data blocks are used to store the actual file data in the file system. Generally each inode contains 13 data block address slots. The
first eight address slots point at the first eight file data blocks of the
file. The ninth address points to an incore inode structure. The disk
inode information is copied to this structure when the file is opened.
The 10th through 13th addresses point to *indirect data blocks* that are
used to address data blocks for large files. Each indirect block supports 1024 addresses. Newer UNIX file systems may incorporate
additional structures to represent much larger files and file systems.

Directory Structure

The UNIX directory and file structure is organized such that it
resembles an inverted tree, beginning with the root directory at the
top and subdirectory branches proceeding down from the root.
Each directory level in the tree may contain files or additional sub-
directories. Directories also act as mount points for connecting
additional file systems to the tree. The root-level directory, designated "/", acts as the base mount point for the full tree structure. A
listing of mounted file systems, their mount points and attributes
can be displayed using the df command (Example 2.6). When
perusing the mount information on various systems you may recog-
nize a set of common directory names. There is a somewhat standard set of directories used to house various types of files. These are
listed in Table 2.7.

Example 2.6 *Mounted Filesystem Attributes*

```
# df
Filesystem   512-blocks  Free    %Used   Iused   %Iused  Mounted on
/dev/hd4     131072      81496   38%     2302    15%     /
/dev/hd2     1310720     91144   94%     25779   16%     /usr
/dev/hd9var  262144      156592  41%     554     2%      /var
/dev/hd3     524288      307744  42%     335     1%      /tmp
/dev/lv01    786432      219952  73%     7442    8%      /home
/dev/lv02    1507328     236704  85%     14707   32%     /usr/local
```

Table 2.7   *Common UNIX Directories*

/	Root of filesystem tree
/bin	Command binary files
/dev	Device files
/etc	Configuration files and administrative scripts
/home	User files
/lib, /usr/lib	Library files
/sbin	System binary files
/tmp	Temporary files
/usr/bin	Commands and scripts
/usr/adm	Accounting and administrative files
/usr/include	System ".h" include files
/var, /usr/spool	Spool and log files
/usr/local	Local commands, scripts, and files
/usr/man	Manual pages

File Interface

In the opening paragraphs of this chapter I mentioned that all UNIX objects are abstracted as files. This interface provides a common set of system calls which can be used to manipulate file objects. It also allows for chaining together the various file I/O commands and system calls from programs, shell scripts, and the command line. As one might expect there are some subtle differences in the interfaces based on the attributes of the target file object (Table 2.8). This will be useful information to keep in mind when attempting to operate on UNIX file objects via a Samba shared directory.

Table 2.8   *UNIX File types*

Regular	Byte strings that have no imposed structure
Directories	Paired list of inodes and filenames
Hard Links	Files referenced by more than one name within the same file system
Symbolic Links	File name pointer to a file residing in any file system

continued on next page

Table 2.8   *continued*

Block	/dev file that points to block data device driver
Character	/dev file that points to a character data device driver
Named Pipes	SYSV channel for interprocess communication
Socket	BSD channel for interprocess communication

File type and permitted operation attribute information can be displayed using the ls command (Example 2.7). The leftmost column in the long option of the command indicates the file type by the first character in the string. The subsequent set of r, w, and x characters specify the respective read, write, and execute permissions for the owner, group and world. The owner and group are listed as strings in the next set of columns preceding size, date, and file name.

Example 2.7   *File Attributes and Permissions*

```
# ls al⊢ /home/deroest
total 1152
drwx-rx-rx    4 deroest   system   1024 Nov 14 04:45   ./
drwx-rx-rx    5 bin       bin       512 Aug 08 16:08   ../
-rw-------    1 deroest   system    150 Aug 12 04:56   .Xauthority
drwx-rx-rx    8 deroest   system    512 Aug 12 04:56   .dt/
-rwx-rx-rx    1 deroest   system   3970 Aug 12 04:56   .dtprofile*
-rwxr-----    1 deroest   system    254 Aug 08 16:08   .profile*
-rw-----      1 deroest   system     54 Sep 26 07:43   .sh_history
drwx-rx-rx    4 deroest   system    512 Sep 26 07:42   info/
```

NFS

A common way of sharing files and directories between networked UNIX systems is Sun's *Network File System (NFS)*. NFS is a stateless file sharing protocol based on a set of *Remote Procedure Calls (RPCs)* and an *External Data Representation (XDR)* specification to trap, reroute, and communicate file operations and attributes between machines. NFS is based on a client/server architecture that enables applications to interoperate seamlessly on remote files and directories without regard to their locale. Sun placed this architecture in the public domain and it became a de facto standard for distributed file systems under UNIX. NFS is also supported on many other operating systems including Windows. Again, it is important to understand NFS and its relationship to Samba directory shares in mixed environments.

NFS servers rely on a number of daemons to manage distributed file system services (Table 2.9). I/O requests from multiple clients are multiplexed through a configurable number of nfsd and biod daemons. The nfsd daemons manage file I/O operations and the biod daemons control block I/O services. NFS servers register themselves with the portmap daemon which maintains the list of RPC applications on a particular machine. Client applications query the portmap daemon to determine the port number associated with a known service name. The rpc.mountd daemon is used by the server to manage and track client mount requests. Recent RPC operations between clients and servers are cached by the rpc.statd daemon. SYSV advisory file and record locking is supported by the server's rpc.lockd daemon.

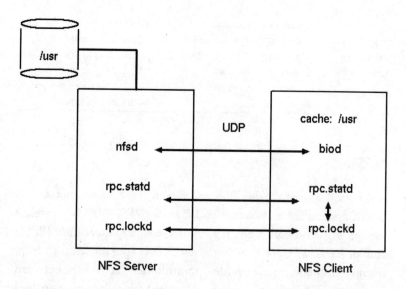

Figure 2.4   *NFS client to server interface*

Table 2.9   *NFS Server Daemons*

nfsd	NFS server daemon
biod	NFS block I/O daemon
portmap	RPC program to port manager
rpc.mountd	NFS mount manager
rpc.statd	RPC status manager
rpc.lockd	NFS lock manager

Each file system or directory available for remote mounting is identified with an entry in the server's /etc/exports file (Example 2.8). Along with the directory path name, the /etc/exports entry controls which machine names are allowed to mount the directory, operate on it with root permissions whether there is read-only or write access. If NFS root access is not enabled for a remote NFS client, the root UID of the server is mapped to a default UID of –2 (4294967294), user name *nobody*. This restricts compromises by unknown superuser UIDs on remote machines.

Example 2.8   */etc/exports entry*

```
/usr/lpp/info/En_US -ro,access=alph,lisa
/home -rw,root=alph,access=alph,lisa,armada
```

Printing

Printing is fairly straightforward under UNIX given the file I/O abstraction for interoperating with devices. In the simplest form an ASCII character file can be printed by piping the file into the device file representing a local printer.

```
# cat myfile | /dev/lp.
```

To facilitate print queuing for local and remote printers, the lpd daemon comes into play. When started, lpd digests printer and queue definitions listed in the /etc/printcap file (Example 2.9). The printcap file specifies all the attributes associated with each printer and queue. This includes whether banner and/or trailer pages are printed, if special back-end drivers or filters are required for the device, what access controls are in force, and whether accounting information should be logged. In the case of a remote queue, the remote site is identified.

Example 2.9   */etc/printcap*

```
# Sample printcamp
lp|Sample Printer Entry:\
        :lp=/dev/null:\
        :sd=/var/spool/lpd/lp0:\
        :if=/usr/local/lib/your-input-filter:\
        :rm=host.your.domain.com:\
        :mx#0:
```

Access Control

The /etc/passwd and /etc/group files form the foundation of access control in UNIX. In general the right to operate on an object is governed by ownership or membership in a group associated with the object. Newer versions of UNIX have augmented access control mechanisms by including support for *Access Control Lists (ACL).* ACLs allow finer granularity than do operations allowed on an object and permit the end-user to set up and control custom groups. On the downside, ACLs are not easily mapped between environments and may not work over remote file shares.

Passwords

The UNIX password file, /etc/passwd, is a table which identifies all users permitted to log-in to the system (Example 2.10). Each user account is assigned a text string *Account Name* and a numeric identifier, called a **UID**, which is unique to the individual computer. Another numeric identifier associated with the user is a default group identifier, **GID**. Basically the UID and GID tags are used by the system in managing access control. The password file may or may not include the encrypted password for the user population. Because the password file is visible to all users, some systems have moved the encrypted passwords into a restricted access file called the *shadow password* file. This defeats the ability to use the visible password file easily by password cracking programs. When shadow passwords are in effect a place holder character, *!*, is inserted into the password field in /etc/passwd indicating that the associated encrypted password can be found in the shadow password file. Other information in the password file may include personal name and address data in the *gecos* field, the user's *home directory*, and the default *shell*. Each field in the password file is separated by a colon.

```
Accout Name:!:UID:GID:<Gecos strings>:<Home
     Directory>:<Shell>
```

Example 2.10   */etc/passwd*

```
root:!:0:0:System Overseer:/:/bin/ksh
daemon:!:1:1::/etc:
bin:!:2:2::/bin:
sys:!:3:3::/usr/sys:
adm:!:4:4::/usr/adm:
uucp:!:5:5::/usr/lib/uucp:
stimpy:!:4084:30:Stimpson Cat:/u1/stimpy:/bin/ksh
```

Parsing large password files can cause significant delays in command response time. To improve response time some UNIX implementations support mirroring /etc/passwd information in an indexed set of dbm databases. The mkpasswd command reads /etc/passwd and creates the keyed directory file, /etc/passwd.dir, and a data file, /etc/passwd.pag. Password dbm support is not required, but is provided as an option for sites with large user communities.

```
# mkpasswd /etc/passwd    Create new passwd dbm database.
```

Groups

Groups provide a coarse mechanism for sharing information between users. Similar to the /etc/passwd file, the /etc/group file is a table that identifies all the group names on the system, the associated GID, and a comma-separated list of the account names that make up the group membership (Example 2.11). UNIX assumes a limited group set to implement default access privileges. The system administrator can add users to these default groups or create new ones to facilitate additional collaborations. If the user base is small, this can be done relatively easily. For large numbers of users, managing GID sets can be a big chore.

Example 2.11   */etc/group*

```
system:!:0:root,ops
daemon:!:1:
bin:!:2:root,bin
sys:!:3:root,bin,sys
adm:!:4:bin,adm,kenm,root
uucp:!:5:uucp
mail:!:6:
security:!:7:root
cron:!:8:root
staff:!:10:root,ren,stimpy,daffy,huey,dewey
user:!:30:luge,acadmus,gwyneira,bungi
```

Network Information Service

The *Network Information Service (NIS)* is an administrative tool that can be used to distribute common system configuration information between machines. NIS and NIS+ are what was commonly known as "Yellow Pages (YP)." NIS is a real boon to system administrators charged with maintaining a large number of machines in a lab or distributed network. The collection of participating machines is called the *NIS domain*. Each file in the distribution set is converted into ndbm database format and stored as an *NIS map* file on the server. The collection of NIS maps makes up the *NIS database* which is distributed periodically to the machines in the NIS domain.

As you may have guessed, two files commonly distributed using NIS are the /etc/passwd and /etc/group files. NIS provides a convenient method for synchronizing account information across multiple machines. In cases where only a portion of the full set of accounts and groups need to be kept common between machines, NIS allows for segregating the accounts and groups into *local* and *distributed* categories (Table 2.10). Local information is unique to each machine. Distributed information is configuration information administered on the master NIS server and pushed to participating machines for the sake of uniformity. Local data override conflicting distributed data.

Table 2.10   *NIS Password and Group Files*

/etc/passwd
/etc/passwd.yp
/etc/passwd.local
/etc/group
/etc/group.yp
/etc/group.local

Kerberos

There are a number of authentication systems available for UNIX, which augment the functionality and security of the basic password and group architecture. One such system is the *Kerberos* authentication developed at M.I.T., which is based on the *Trusted Third-Party* authentication model. The original design is described in a series of papers presented at the 1988 USENIX Winter Conference. Kerberos is an important technology regarding UNIX and NT coexistence, because it is the network authentication system in Windows 2000.

Kerberos assumes that everything in the network is untrustworthy except the Kerberos authentication server itself. The Kerberos authentication server is called the *Key Distribution Center (KDC)*. The KDC acts as an intermediary between the client and the desired services. The client must authenticate itself to the KDC to obtain a ticket, which grants the rights to access distributed services (Figure 2.5). This ticket is called a *Ticket Granting Ticket (TGT)*. It is only necessary to validate yourself once to the KDC rather than once for each service you wish to access. The various Kerberos tick-

ets are also only valid for a given period of time. The Kerberos ticket mechanism eliminates the need to transmit passwords over the
network in clear text. The client and server passwords are known
and stored by the KDC.

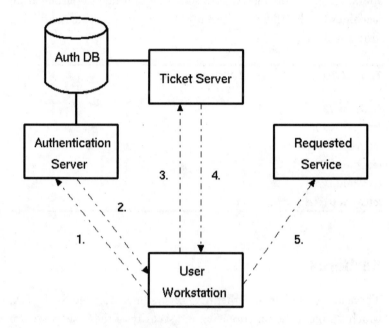

1. Request authentication for user and service.
2. Return TS session key and identifiers.
3. Request ticket using sealed authenticator.
4. Return ticket for requested service.
5. Connect to service with authenticator ticket.

Figure 2.5   *Kerberos ticket exchange*

   Whenever access to services is requested by an unauthenticated
client, a message is sent to the KDC that contains client name and the
Kerberos ticket-granting service name. The KDC looks up the names
and obtains the *encryption* key for the client and the ticket server. The
encryption key is known only to the owning agent and the KDC. A
message is then constructed by the KDC containing the client and
ticket server names, address, and a random *session key*, which it encrypts

using the client's encryption key. The message is called a *ticket* and is sent to the client. The client uses its encryption key to decrypt the ticket and stores the ticket for the duration for which it is valid. The session key is used to encrypt ticket communication with the Kerberos ticket service to gain access to other services and resources.

When access to a service is requested, the ticket service provides a new session key along with a ticket encrypted with the services encryption key from the KDC's database. The client uses the new session key to create an *authenticator* ticket, which identifies the client, and sends it along with the encrypted service ticket to the new service. The service decrypts the ticket using its encryption key. The service ticket contains the session key, which is then used to decrypt the authenticator ticket. Now the client and service know about each other and real work can begin.

This may seem like a lot of hand waving to inhibit clear text passwords and authentication information from being broadcast over the network. On the other hand, it is extremely easy to eavesdrop on the wire. All this negotiation is taking place under the covers, so it is not visible to the end-user. Remember that Kerberos will not restrict access to someone who has already compromised another user's login ID and password.

Summary

- UNIX has a three-tiered architecture: kernel, shell, and command layers.
- Executing tasks and programs are called *processes* and are identified by *PID* number.
- Server processes are called *daemons*.
- Init, PID 1, is responsible for spawning system processes, which are identified in the **/etc/inittab** file.
- TCP/IP is a network protocol with four layers: *physical, internetwork, transport,* and *application*.
- Each computer on the network is identified by a four-octet IP number.
- Groups of networked computers are partitioned using *subnets* to isolate and manage traffic and to enforce security policies.

- A hierarchical dynamic network name service called the *Domain Name Service (DNS)* resolves domain name to IP numbers.
- The UNIX DNS server is called `named`.
- DNS server addresses are identified in `/etc/resolv.conf`.
- The **inetd** server starts network servers when requested by a client defined as `/etc/inetd.conf`.
- Well-known service name-to-port mapping is recorded in `/etc/services`.
- UNIX file systems are contained in collections of disk blocks called *partitions*.
- File system structure within a partition is represented as the *superblock, inode table,* and *data blocks*.
- File systems contain a hierarchical collection of *files* and *directories*, each of which is recorded in an inode.
- All UNIX objects are abstracted as files.
- File and directory access controls are recorded in the inode indicating *read, write,* and *execute* permissions for *owner, group,* and *world*.
- NFS is a stateless networked file system for sharing files and directories.
- Local and remote printing and queuing is managed by the `lpd` daemon.
- Printer and queue configuration information is recorded in `/etc/printcaps`.
- UNIX users are identified by an *account name, UID* and *GID*.
- User identification information is stored in `/etc/passwd`.
- Restricted access to the encrypted password database is enabled through the use of shadow password files.
- Password access performance can be improved through the use of a `dbm` password database, `/etc/passwd.dir`, and `/etc/passwd.pag`.
- Group authorization is defined in `/etc/groups`.
- *NIS* can be used to distribute password and group information to multiple machines that share a common user base.
- *Kerberos* is a network-based authentication system based on *Trusted Third-Party* model.
- Kerberos authentication is supported in Windows 2000.

Windows Overview

In the last chapter, we looked at various pieces of the UNIX system and networking framework to assist in developing a model for sharing UNIX resources with Windows clients using Samba. In Chapter 3, we continue this discussion thread by examining the corresponding Windows system and networking subsystems. In particular, we will look closely at Windows networking protocols, domains and workgroups, file systems, and access controls. Samba is an implementation of Windows file-and-print sharing services and also provides basic *NT Primary Domain Controller (PDC)* functionality. Thus a sound understanding of Windows networking protocols and domain services will be critical in successfully deploying Samba in the enterprise.

Windows NT Architecture

The Windows NT operating system is similar to UNIX in that processes interact with CPU, memory, and hardware via an executive system services layer. NT employs *preemptive multitasking* to manage the execution of process threads in much the same way UNIX schedulers work. This allows NT to suspend some tasks to provide resources for higher priority tasks. NT is also multithreaded, giving it the capability of running on symmetric multiprocessing platforms. This seems quite a bit like UNIX. The NT development team spent a fair amount of time reviewing and borrowing ideas from UNIX and other computing architectures, and ultimately used Carnegie Mellon's *Mach microkernel* as the foundation for the operating system.

Windows NT is implemented as a layered subsystem architecture and supports applications from a number of different operating system environments (Figure 3.1). In contrast to the previous chapter's bottom-up discussion of the UNIX OS layers, we will view Windows NT from the top down. At the top layer of the NT architecture stack reside *user mode* services. These include a *Virtual DOS Machine (VDM)* for running legacy DOS applications, a *16-bit Windows subsystem* for Windows 3.x programs, a *POSIX subsystem*, an *OS/2 subsystem*, and the *Win32 subsystem*. Applications executing within a particular subsystem are managed as separate protected virtual memory spaces. User mode services interact with lower-level *kernel-mode* services through the *executive services buffer*. This buffer is a code section that partitions and protects user-mode and kernel-mode operations. Immediately below this buffer are the *NT Executive Managers*, which regulate object and process life cycles; virtual memory; procedure calls; I/O functions; and monitor access security. A small fixed *microkernel* sits below the executive manager layer. The microkernel's role is limited to dispatching and synchronizing threads and managing system interrupts. The base of the operating system is made up of the *Hardware Abstraction Layer (HAL)*, whose job is to hide hardware and device-driver dependencies from the rest of the operating system. This simplifies, secures, and generalizes the API for developing applications that use hardware services.

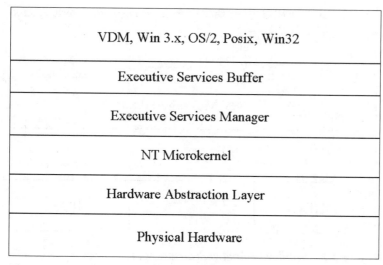

Figure 3.1 *Windows NT layered architecture*

Networking

Windows NT comes complete with almost all the network protocols and interfaces one could ask for (Figure 3.2). The usual suspects
include TCP/IP, NetBIOS/NetBEUI, and IPX/SPX. The base protocols and interfaces are augmented by additional communication
services to support Virtual Private Networking (VPN) and Routing
and Remote Access Services (RRAS), as well as gateway support
among Microsoft LAN Manager, OS2 LAN Manager, Banyan
Vines, Novell, and the Internet. For our purposes, we will narrow
the set down to NetBIOS and TCP/IP, which provide the transport
for the *Server Message Block (SMB)* protocol between Samba and
Windows clients and servers.

NetBIOS

A long time ago, in a LAN far, far away, an API was developed to
extend the *Basic Input/Output System (BIOS)* services of personal
computers to include support for sharing information between computers over a network. The resulting *NetBIOS* API is documented in
the *IBM PC Network Technical Reference Manual*, (September 1994).

The NetBIOS API defines three service types: *session service, datagram service*, and *name service*.

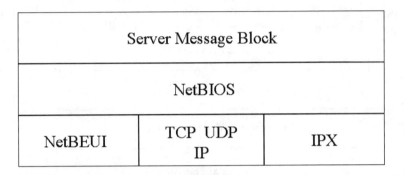

Server Message Block		
NetBIOS		
NetBEUI	TCP UDP IP	IPX

Figure 3.2   *Windows NT network architecture*

Conversations between NetBIOS applications are facilitated by NetBIOS session and datagram services. The NetBIOS session service is used when a reliable virtual circuit with guaranteed delivery is required for passing messages between two known parties. An example of a session-based connection would be accessing a file share. In contrast, the NetBIOS datagram service is used for connectionless communication without guaranteed delivery when the target recipient is not known in advance. Datagrams, or *Mailslots* in the Microsoft parlance, are usually transmitted as network broadcasts or multicasts to a group of machines. Datagram services are used when a client requests the identification of the master browser.

NetBT

NetBIOS itself is not a communications protocol, but a programming interface for establishing and managing network-based services. Messages between NetBIOS applications must be carried over the network by a transport-layer protocol. Popular transport protocols include NetBEUI, IPX, DECNet, and TCP/IP. Samba uses *NetBIOS over TCP/IP (NetBT)* as defined in RFCs 1001 and 1002 as its transport service. As we shall see later in the chapter, the use of NetBT as a transport is critical when scaling NetBIOS services in large networks.

Name Service

NetBIOS name service is represented as a flat, non-hierarchical namespace. Each service entry is identified by a 16-byte string that constitutes either a unique name for the service or the group name of which it is a member (Figure 3.3). The first 15 bytes of the string represent the alphanumeric machine or group name. The 16th byte is a hexadecimal number that indicates the machine's or group's resource type (Table 3.1).

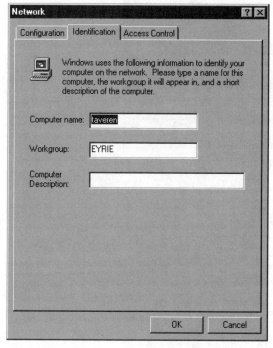

Figure 3.3   *Setting NetBIOS name and workgroup*

Conflicts between resource names residing within the same logical subnet or workgroup can be resolved by partitioning the namespace through the use of a NetBIOS *scope* identifier (Figure 3.4). This is a character string used in conjunction with the NetBIOS name to enforce uniqueness in the namespace. The total length of the NetBIOS scope plus the NetBIOS name cannot exceed 256 characters. Note that the use of NetBIOS scopes effectively isolates resources from communicating with each other.

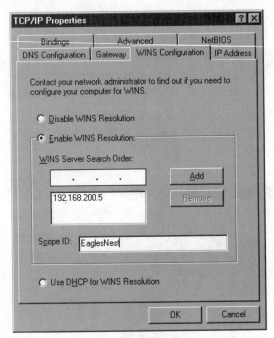

Figure 3.4   *Setting NetBIOS scope*

Table 3.1   *NetBIOS Names*

Characters 1-15:   Machine or Group Name

<a-z, A-Z, 0-9, !, @, #, $, %, ^, &, (,), -, *, ', { }, ., ~>

Character 16:	Unique Resource Type
<00>	Workstation Service Name
<03>	Messenger Service Name
<06>	RAS Server
<1B>	Domain Master Browser
<1F>	NetDDE Service
<20>	Server Service
<21>	RAS Client
<BE>	Network Monitor Agent
<BF>	Network Monitor Utility

continued on next page

Table 3.1 *NetBIOS Names*

Group Resource Type	
<1C>	Domain Group Name
<1D>	Master Browser Name
<1E>	Group Name for Elections
<20>	Internet Group

Each application registers its presence in the namespace by making a NetBIOS Add Name or Add Group Name call. The service or group name is then reserved in the namespace until specifically released by a Delete call or the machine on which the service resides is shut down. Registered names and resource types can be queried by invoking the Windows nbtstat command. In Example 3.1, nbtstat is used to display the registered NetBIOS resource table for a machine named *Wizard*. The listing indicates that Wizard is a member of the group *Eyrie* and it has one connected user, *DeRoest*. The reserved name _MSBROWSE_ delineates Wizard as the registered master browser for the group.

Example 3.1 *NetBIOS Machine Listing*

```
C:\nbtstat -a Wizard
NetBIOS Remote Machine Name Table

Name               Type            Status
---------------------------------------------------
WIZARD             <00> UNIQUE     Registered
EYRIE              <00> GROUP      Registered
WIZARD             <03> UNIQUE     Registered
WIZARD             <20> UNIQUE     Registered
EYRIE              <1E> GROUP      Registered
DEROEST            <03> UNIQUE     Registered
EYRIE              <1D> UNIQUE     Registered
.._MSBROWSE__..    <01> GROUP      Registered
```

NetBIOS name service uses two methods for registering, resolving, and releasing NetBIOS names, groups, and addresses. The first method administers the namespace using network broadcasts. The client machine queries or announces a name on the network as a broadcast and then waits for a response to the request. Because delivery is not guaranteed, the client may have to retransmit its request a number of times before it is resolved. This method works in small networks but quickly breaks down on large networks due to heavy broadcast traffic.

The second method for managing the namespace uses point-to-point communication. Name registration and IP address resolution requests are directed to a *NetBIOS Name Server (NBNS)* in a manner similar to Internet dynamic DNS. NetBIOS point-to-point name service is defined in RFC 1001 and RFC 1002 and implemented as Microsoft's *Windows Internet Name Service (WINS)* (Figure 3.5).

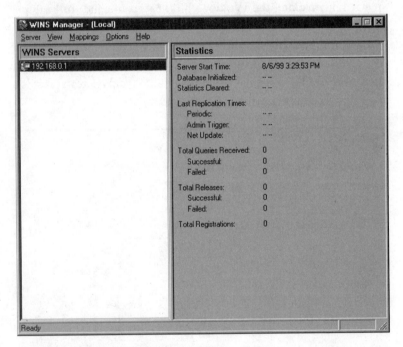

Figure 3.5   *WINS configuration*

NetBIOS name-to-IP address mappings can also be hard coded in *LMHOSTS* tables and stored on each machine. The LMHOSTS table is a flat ASCII file of IP address and name pairs. If both WINS and LMHOSTS information are available for resolving names, clients will first consult their local NetBIOS cache and then WINS before using LMHOSTS information. It is also possible to prime the client NetBIOS cache at system startup with LMHOSTS entries that have been flagged as #PRE (Example 3.2).

Example 3.2 *LMHOSTS Stanza*

```
149.110.5.12   Wizard  #PRE
```

The broadcast and point-to-point capabilities of various LAN clients for name-to-address resolution are based on their node type as defined in Table 3.2.

Table 3.2 *Name Resolution Methods*

Node Type	Name Resolution Method
B-NODE	Broadcast to resolve names. Uses a mixture of directed and broadcast UDP and TCP for resolving name. All network nodes must listen for broadcasts.
P-NODE	Point-to-point only node. Uses directed UDP and TCP connections. Relies on access to name server to resolve names.
M-NODE	Mixed node. Tries broadcast first and then point-to-point with name server if no response to broadcast.
H-NODE	Hybrid node. Tries point-to-point first and then falls back to broadcast if the name server cannot be contacted.
MS ENHANCED	Same as an H-NODE but will also use the LMHOSTS file.

Server Message Block (SMB)

Thus far, we have taken a brief look at MS Windows network services and protocols at the network, transport, and to a limited degree, the session layer. Now we are ready to move higher in the stack and probe the *Server Message Block (SMB)* protocol, which is where Samba lives and breathes (Figure 3.2). SMB is a session-, presentation-, and application-layer protocol that provides a means for remotely sharing files, printers, and various communication resources between networked computers. The SMB protocol was first defined in a joint Microsoft and Intel document titled *Microsoft Networks/OpenNET-File Sharing Protocol* in 1987. Early SMB implementations included MS LAN Manager in 1987 and OS/2 LAN Server in 1988. In 1992 SMB became an Open Group interoperability standard, "Protocols for X/Open PC Interworking: SMB, Version 2, X/Open CAE Specification C209." Microsoft, in collaboration with a number of computing and networking vendors, defined an enhanced version of SMB under a new title, the *Common Internet File System (CIFS)* protocol. CIFS version 1.0 has been submitted as a draft to the *Internet Engineering Task Force (IETF)* for consideration as an informational RFC.

SMB is a connection-oriented protocol implemented on the NetBIOS API. The protocol provides a mechanism for Windows consumer and server applications to communicate in a request/response manner over a virtual circuit. The internal structure of each server message block is represented as a string of Intel format multi-byte values ordered least significant byte first. Each block begins with a fixed-length header, followed by a variable set of parameter fields, and finishes with a data buffer. The SMB command protocol can essentially be broken down into four types of operations; *session*, *file*, *printer*, and *message*. SMB session commands are used to set up a virtual circuit and validate access. File and printer commands permit an application to operate on files and spool jobs to remote printers. Message commands provide a means for passing alert, control, and informational messages between the consumer and server applications. The simplified SMB session described in Example 3.3 will give a feel for how SMB sessions are set up and released.

Example 3.3   *SMB Session*

SMBnegprot	Initial message listing dialects supported by the consumer application. Server responds with selected dialect.
SMBsesssetup	The application's credentials are passed for verification. Server responds with UID.
SMBtcon	Indicates the name of the share requested by the client. Server responds with TID of share.

continued on next page

Example 3.3 *SMB Session*

SMBopen	File name to open. Server responds with FID to be used in subsequent file operations.
SMBread	TID, FID, offset, and number of bytes to read.
SMBclose	Close file FID in share TID.
SMBtdis	Disconnect from share TID.

The initial negotiation of SMB dialect in the example is required due to extensions in the protocol that have occurred over its development history. The base level SMB version is known as the "core protocol." Other dialects are listed in Table 3.3. Samba supports SMB at the CIFS 1.0 and Windows NT LAN Manager 0.12 level.

Table 3.3 *SMB Dialects*

PC Network Program 1.0	Core Protocol
Microsoft Networks 1.03	Core plus Protocol
Microsoft Networks 3.0	Extended 1.0 Protocol

One of the features of newer versions of the SMB protocol is that it supports *opportunistic locking* or *oplocks*. By acquiring an oplock on a file an SMB application can read ahead and buffer data locally for updates, thus improving performance. There are three types of oplocks. Acquisition of an *Exclusive oplock* means that no other application can read or modify the target file. The lock holder has exclusive control over the file. A *Batch oplock* allows an application to maintain a lock on the file through successive opens and closes, thus reducing network traffic between the client and server. A *Level II oplock* permits multiple applications to read a file but not update it.

Common Internet File System (CIFS)

As mentioned earlier, CIFS is an enhanced version of the SMB protocol. Along with being backwards-compatible with SMB, CIFS provides a means for sharing resources between multiple OS platforms across the Internet. This is accomplished through the use of HTTP URL-like resource location semantics and Internet DNS. In regard to scalability and fault tolerance, CIFS supports multiple writers to a single file through aggressive locking and caching algorithms. With its intent to support resource sharing in a larger community, CIFS can adapt to a wide range of network speeds. This includes everything from slow dial-up modem bit rates to gigabit backbone connections. Unicode character sets are also employed with the wider Internet audience in mind.

Peers, Workgroups, Domains, Forests

One of the first things that comes to mind when planning a networking infrastructure for resource sharing is how to control access to those resources.

Workgroups

In a small homogenous MS Windows environment, it might be possible to operate on a friendly peer-to-peer basis. You let me play with your toys and I'll think about letting you play with mine. This type of environment is usually implemented as a *workgroup* (Figure 3.6). Workgroups provide a means of grouping together users and resources that share a common work profile. Workgroups also simplify the task of locating resources in the network. It may not be necessary to browse for a particular resource on each and every workstation on the network, because it may be that the resource is known to reside in a particular workgroup, thus reducing the number of systems to be checked.

Each user in the workgroup usually has autonomous control over the resources on the desktop. A user can assign passwords to local resources to limit access under *share-level* security (Figure 3.7). Share-level security regulates access by requiring knowledge of the appropriate password. Access control by user and group is called *user level*. This requires the presence of a Windows NT computer that acts as a security server. The absence of a security server in the workgroup model means that each user must have an account and password stored locally on each of the workgroup computers used. It also means that each user must know all the passwords required to access the various resources available in the local or remote workgroups. Workgroups may seem like an administrative nightmare, but it is possible for a system administrator to exert some level of control over resource sharing through the use of system policies and profiles. Password management will most likely remain problem.

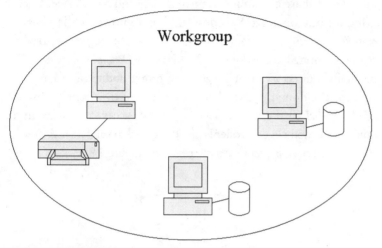

Figure 3.6 *Workgroup model*

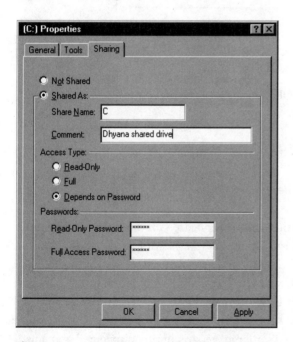

Figure 3.7 *Setting share level passwords*

Domains

Centralized management of accounts, passwords, and shares can be more easily realized by implementing a Windows *domain* model for the network. A Windows domain is a logical collection of users and computers that share a common security policy and namespace. In each domain, one or more Windows NT computers, called *domain controllers*, act as a locus for administering and resolving access to all the resources located in the domain. The *Primary Domain Controller (PDC)* maintains a directory of all the account, group, and password information for the domain. This directory is called the *Security Accounts Manager (SAM)*. To log in to a computer or access a resource in the domain, the domain controller is first consulted to validate user credentials before access is granted to the resource (Figure 3.8).

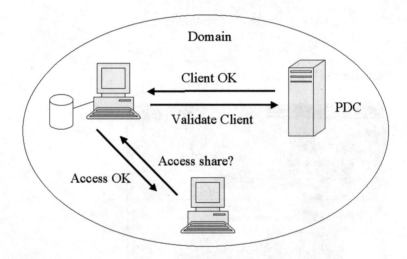

Figure 3.8   *Simple domain model*

SAM information can be replicated on one or more additional domain controllers called *Backup Domain Controllers (BDC)*. The presence of a BDC assists in ensuring fault tolerance for the SAM directory. A BDC will also respond to a validation request at times when the PDC is busy or unavailable due to a system or network failure. The existence of a BDC is not required, but it should be carefully considered for large, geographically distributed domains.

Trust

In instances when an organization's business rules, administrative structure, or geographic layout doesn't neatly fit the single domain model, multiple domains can be set up and logically connected through *trust* relationships. Users in a trusted domain are allowed to access resources and participate in group membership in the local domain without having to duplicate SAM directory entries in both domains. This feature provides a means for distributing namespace administration functions in large enterprises.

Trust relationships can be broken down into three models, *one-way trust*, *two-way trust*, and *complete trust*. In a one-way trust model, domain A permits access to local resources by domain B, but domain B does not return the favor by permitting access to its resources. In a two-way trust environment, access to resources in domains A and B are permitted in both directions. In the complete-trust model, all domains have access to all resources, no matter where they are located. Complete trust or combinations with the other models are very difficult to manage.

Domain Models

The ability to replicate the SAM directory and define trust relationships between domains provides a great deal of flexibility in designing a robust and scalable infrastructure. In reality, the sky is the limit concerning domain topologies. However, there are three common domain models that may be useful in planning an environment.

The simplest model is the *single domain* infrastructure described previously. All participating resources are members of a single domain. The domain has one PDC and may have one or more computers acting as BDCs. This model is the easiest to administer but may be awkward for large numbers of users or machines.

To facilitate management of large populations of users and resources, yet maintain a single domain for the user namespace, it is possible to separate administration of the SAM directory and resources into separate domains. This model is called the *master domain* model, and it maintains the SAM directory. One or more *resource domains* are defined to manage shares. A one-way trust relationship is defined to allow users in the master domain to access the shares in the resource domains. This model supports central administration of the user namespace and allows for local administration of shares in the resource domains.

In large distributed organizations, it may make more sense to partition the namespace to support localized administration of user accounts and resources. This *multi-master domain* model represents the opposite end of the spectrum from the single domain model. The namespace is broken up into administrative units, each with its own security policy and definitions. Trust relationships are established as needed to facilitate interoperability between domains. As mentioned in the discussion on trust, this model is the most difficult to manage and requires close coordination between domain administrators.

Trees and Forests

Windows 2000 builds upon the domain model by organizing domains into a hierarchical tree structure supporting both central and distributed administration (Figure 3.9). It also increases the maximum namespace size to 10,000,000 objects. Windows NT 3.5 only supports 10,000 objects and Windows NT 4.0 supports 40,000. The collection of domains and administrative policies is managed by Windows 2000 *Active Directory*, a combination of the legacy NT domain security architecture augmented with a set of open technologies that include *Lightweight Directory Access Protocol (LDAP)*, Kerberos Version 5.0, and Internet-style *Domain Name Service (DNS)*. Active Directory supports a mixed environment of Windows 2000 and Windows NT 4.0 domain controllers. Back-level clients can still log in using NT LAN Manager challenge/response authentication.

An Active Directory *tree* is a hierarchy of domains that represents a contiguous namespace with a common *LDAP schema* and *Kerberos transitive trust* relationships. A schema defines the attributes associated with each object in the namespace. Kerberos trust is similar to the domain trust relationships we have already described. A group of trees which share common schema and trust relationships can be grouped into a larger administrative unit called a *forest*. Like domains, Active Directory tree and forest information, called the *global catalog*, is replicated across multiple servers, but in a multi-master topology versus the primary and backup model used by domains.

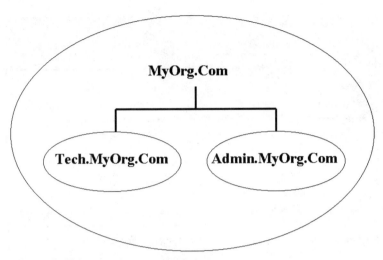

Figure 3.9   *Active Directory domain tree*

Active Directory augments the domain trust model by overlaying a domain tree with an independent structure called an *Organizational Unit (OU)* tree. An OU is a container that holds network objects including users, groups, shares, and other OUs. Individual OU security attributes are defined by the Active Directory schema. OUs provide a finer degree of administrative authority that is independent of domain boundaries. An individual domain might implement an OU tree within the domain to distribute administrative functions to subgroups in the domain. A central IT department might define a global OU that covers all domains to centralize administration of the namespace.

Browsing

Workstations locate shares by browsing. Basically, browsing is akin to window shopping in a large mall or shopping center. We go from one network computer store to the next, looking to see what resources might be available for use (Figure 3.10). There are two categories of browsers, *browser clients* and *browser servers*. Clients query browser servers to locate resources. Grouping resources by domain or workgroup limits browsing scope and simplifies the task of locating the desired resource.

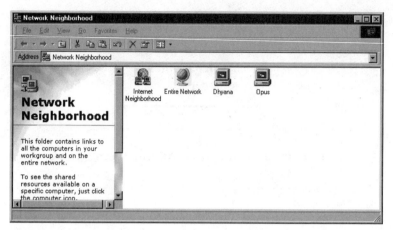

Figure 3.10   *Browsing the network neighborhood*

Each subnet within a domain has a *local master browser* to localize browsing traffic. Servers within the domain register their shares with the local master. The subnet local master is elected from the candidate computers within a domain, via a dynamic bid process. Each computer bids by announcing its operating system level, revision, and desired browser role as a four-byte string called its *election criteria* (Table 3.4). The computer with the highest election criteria wins the election and announces its claim to victory. Other contenders are demoted to *backup browser* status to support redundancy and load sharing. The election process is called when a client believes that the local master has failed or is unavailable.

Each domain also has a *domain master browser* whose responsibility is to synchronize the share datasets between all the local master browsers. The domain master is the collection point for intersubnet browsing. The domain PDC always acts as the domain master browser. In single-subnet domains, the PDC is the domain master browser and local master browser.

Table 3.4 *Browser Election Credentials*

OS Level (Summary)	
Windows for Workgroups	0x01
Windows NT Workstation	0x10
Windows NT Server	0x20

Desired Role	
Backup Browser	0x01
Standby Browser	0x02
Master Browser	0x04
Domain Master Browser	0x08
WINS Client	0x20
Windows NT Server	0x80

File Systems

When it comes to file systems, MS Windows is the 24-flavors ice cream shop of operating systems. Popular flavors include FAT, FAT16, FAT32, OS/2 HPFS, NTFS, and DFS. Then there are the UNIX interoperability flavors: NFS and Samba. Windows provides a great deal of functionality in supporting legacy and contemporary file systems. This capability is especially useful in heterogeneous environments, regardless of whether there are multiple versions of Windows or a mixture of Windows and other operating systems.

FAT

The *file allocation table (FAT)* file system represents the basic common denominator for file and directory support across the family of Windows platforms. The FAT architecture is essentially an indexed table that references data containers called *clusters* within a *partition* of contiguous space on a disk. A cluster represents the smallest unit of storage on a disk. Cluster size ranges from 512 to 32K bytes depending on disk size and format. Because cluster size represents the smallest container for a file or directory, it may be important to tailor the file system and drive format to meet the file size profile for a particular data set.

FAT file systems are defined by four control areas. The first or *reserve area* contains the boot sector, bootstrap program, and partition table. The next area is the *FAT index* of clusters, followed by the *root directory table*, which is a directory of files and top level directories. The fourth area is the *file area* collection of clusters where data are stored.

FAT architecture has evolved over the years in keeping with the availability of larger disks and the demand for larger file sizes. Basically, this has meant an increase in the number of bits in the FAT used to index clusters. More index bits means more clusters can be addressed. Originally the FAT architecture used 12 bits as a cluster index. In DOS 4.0 the index size was increased to 16 bits. In the second release of Windows 95, the FAT index grew once again to 32 bits in *FAT32*.

NTFS

Windows NT introduced another player in the suite of Windows file systems, the *New Technology File System (NTFS)*. In keeping with NT's role as a workgroup or domain server, NTFS provides a scalable and recoverable file system environment to better support and secure server data. NTFS again extended the cluster index to 64 bits. This allows NTFS to address large RAID-based data sets that span multiple disk drives. The structural contents and state of NTFS is tracked and maintained in a relational database called the *master file table (MFT)*. MFT information, along with redundant copies of critical file system data and optional file system mirroring, improves NTFS fault tolerance over FAT file systems and enables automated recovery in the event of a system failure. NTFS also provides enhanced data security over FAT. Access controls can be applied at the individual file level. FAT file systems only apply access controls at the directory level.

DFS

It is often difficult to locate directory shares in medium to large domains. Microsoft's *Distributed File System (DFS)* was introduced to simplify locating directory shares and to provide users with a consistent hierarchical view of available resources. Under DFS, shares residing on a number of servers can be organized into a single directory tree called a *DFS tree*. As client computers traverse the directory tree, they are automatically directed to the server providing the share which makes up that portion of the DFS tree. Alternate directory paths can be defined within DFS to load-balance access to popular shares by replicating the share across multiple servers. When used in conjunction with Windows 2000, LDAP services in Active Directory can be used to identify DFS tree servers for clients. DFS is an add-on service for Windows NT share servers and a client add-on for Windows 9x.

Printing

Windows printers can be network-shared with other computers in a workgroup or domain in much the same way that directories are shared. A physical printer is first defined on the server via a simple Add Printer Wizard. The new printer is associated with the appropriate device driver and is then represented in the system by a virtual printer object and queue. Note that multiple physical print devices called a *printer pool* may be referenced by a single queue name. Once the printer definition is complete, the printer can be assigned a share name and made available for remote access.

The remote client uses the same printer definition wizard and selects "network printer" as the target. If the target server installed the network client driver for the particular printer, the driver will be automatically downloaded from the server and installed on the client. After installation is complete, the network printer can be used by applications just as if it were a local device.

For the local application or user, there is little discernible difference between a local or remote printer. Documents to be printed on a particular device are routed into the associated queue name and processed by the print server process (Figure 3.11). If the destination is a remote share, the document is transferred to the remote site by the network redirector, otherwise it is routed to the local device.

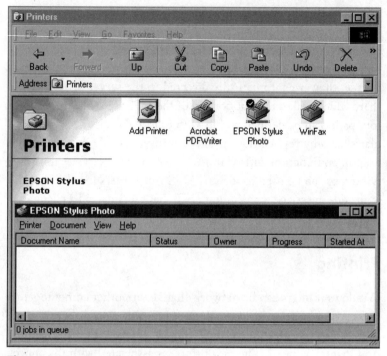

Figure 3.11   *Printer queue listing*

Access Control

In the previous section on domains we talked about how domain user and group credentials and rights are stored in the domain controller's *Security Account Manager (SAM)* database. *Rights* are rules that govern access to all the resources in the domain. Rights can be defined per individual or to groups of individuals that share similar needs (Figure 3.12). Group rights have both local and global scope. Membership in a global group permits access to resources that reside in multiple domains. Global group rights are governed by the interdomain trust relationships. Local groups are restricted to resources within a single domain. Access may also be limited by local SAM information that exists on nondomain controllers and NT workstations.

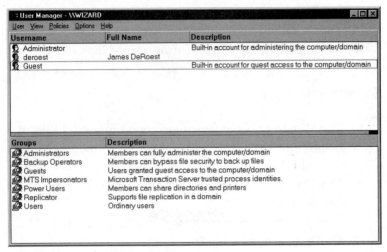

Figure 3.12 *User Manager for domains*

The *Local Security Authority (LSA)* and *Net Login* service are responsible for verifying access rights to resources and authenticating login requests respectively. The LSA validates each request by checking the user's *Resource Identifier (RID)* and the domain's *Security Identifier (SID)* against the access permissions of the requested resource. Resource permissions are defined by *Access Control Lists (ACLs)*.

Kerberos

Windows 2000 enhances the SAM/LSA mechanism by integrating Kerberos 5.0 for network authentication. This third-party authentication system described in the previous chapter on UNIX, is a component of Windows 2000 Active Directory. Kerberos provides additional interoperability between Windows and a number of other vendor operating systems and applications that support the MIT Kerberos specification. Note that Kerberos is an authentication system and does not normally indicate authorization information. Microsoft has enhanced Kerberos by incorporating Windows access control information into an unused field within the Kerberos ticket. The field is ignored by MIT Kerberos systems and does not affect overall interoperability. Windows 2000 clients can be configured to use an MIT Kerberos security server for authentication. Under this configuration, authorization information is collected from Windows 2000 servers via Kerberos transitive trust relationships.

Summary

- The Windows NT operating system represents a layered architecture with partitioned user and kernel modes similar to those of UNIX.
- The Windows NT microkernel was based on the Mach microkernel.
- Common Windows networking protocols include TCP/IP, NetBEUI, and IPX.
- NetBIOS is an API designed to facilitate development of LAN based resource sharing applications. NetBIOS is not a protocol and requires the use of a network transport.
- NetBIOS-over-TCP/IP, called NetBT, is used by Samba to share UNIX resources with Windows clients.
- NetBIOS share names are registered and queried in either of two modes: network broadcast or point-to-point communication with a name server.
- WINS is Microsoft's implementation of a NetBT name server.
- SMB and the subsequent CIFS are NetBT-based resource sharing and messaging protocols. Samba is an implementation of CIFS version 1.0.
- There are many dialects of SMB and CIFS that must be negotiated during session startup.
- Workgroups provide a means of grouping together users and resources that share a common work profile.
- A Windows domain is a logical collection of users and computers sharing a common security policy and namespace.
- In each domain, one or more Windows NT computers, called *domain controllers*, act as a locus for administering and resolving access to all the resources located in the domain.
- The *Primary Domain Controller (PDC)* maintains a directory of all the account, group, and password information for the domain.

- The directory of domain account information is called the *Security Accounts Manager (SAM)*.
- SAM information may be replicated to one or more *Backup Domain Controllers (BDC)*.
- Resources may be shared between domains by defining *trust relationships*.
- Windows 2000 *Active Directory* technology groups domains into hierarchical topologies called *trees* and *forests*.
- Resources within a domain are located via *browsing* services.
- Each subnet within a domain has an elected *local master browser*, which maintains a list of available resources within the subnet.
- The domain PDC acts as a *domain master browser* to synchronize local master browser resource information.
- Windows supports a wide range of file systems including FAT, FAT16, FAT32, OS/2 HPFS, NTFS, and DFS.
- The Microsoft *Distributed File System (DFS)* provides a means of organizing directory shares on multiple computers into a single directory tree.
- Print devices with an associated printer driver are represented as virtual printer objects and referenced by a queue name.
- Multiple physical print devices, called a *printer pool*, may be referenced by a single queue name.
- The *Local Security Authority (LSA)* and *Net Login* service are responsible for verifying access rights to resources and authenticating login requests respectively.
- Resource permissions are definedby *Access Control Lists (ACLs)*.
- Windows 2000 enhances the SAM/LSA mechanism by integrating Kerberos 5.0 for network authentication.

Samba Overview

Samba is a Portuguese word meaning a rhythm and a dance and is derived from the West African Bantu language term *semba*, meaning to pray or invoke the spirits of ancestors. As a Bantu verb *semba* means "to cry" or "the blues." In Brazil, a *Samba* is a woman who is a sacred dancer.

In the world of UNIX, "Samba" is a software suite for remotely sharing UNIX files and printers with networked PCs via the *Server Message Block (SMB)* protocol. SMB is a NetBIOS-based protocol traditionally used in LAN Manager, Windows, and OS/2 networks for accessing remote files and printers, collectively known as *shares* (see Chapter 3). SMB provides a seamless interface between network resources and desktop applications that is often more tightly integrated and transparent than commonly used alternatives like PC-NFS, FTP, and LPR. Samba is a UNIX implementation of SMB-over-TCP/IP (NBT, see RFC 1001 and RFC 1002). From a Windows or LAN Manager desktop perspective, Samba-shared UNIX resources appear just as if they were residing on another Windows or LAN Manager server. No special desktop client software is required. Source code and binary distributions are free to anyone interested in the product. We will cover Samba distribution sites in the next chapter.

Figure 4.1   *Samba home page*

Samba History

Samba is the brainchild of Andrew Tridgell. It all started in December 1991, while he was working as a graduate student in the Computer Sciences Laboratory at Australian National University. According to his own account (see **http://us3.samba.org/samba/ftp/docs/history**), Andrew came up with the idea of trying to reverse-engineer the file-sharing protocol used in Digital Equipment Corporation's Pathworks network for DOS while testing a beta copy of DEC's eXcursion software. eXcursion provides X Windows services for PCs. Testing eXcursion required that he abandon PC-NFS for file sharing and mount disk space using Pathworks. The problem was that Pathworks limited his network file service options to DEC platforms running Ultrix or VMS.

Being an open systems-minded fellow, Andrew decided to eavesdrop on Pathworks network traffic to see if it might be possible to port the protocol to other platforms. This required an extra bit of research on network programming and the building of a software tool to capture network packets off the wire. After poring over the bits and bytes of Pathworks' packet data, he was able to prototype a few basic file operations on a Sun computer he used as a development platform. Additional investigations in the protocol ultimately led him to the NBT RFC literature. Although apparently uncertain how the NBT specification related to his SMB implementation, he continued to refine the code and in January 1992, "Server 0.1" was born.

Over the next few months, Andrew continued porting the software to other non-DEC platforms. This work also included a smattering of bug fixes and additional improvements. The time had come to brand the software with a real version number. "Server 1.0" was ready and subsequently released to the Internet community. Then like any good software development project, the code was left to ferment for a couple of years under public scrutiny.

The project was brought back out of the cobwebs after receiving a note of interest concerning the software from Linux aficionado Dan Shearer. There was also a request from DEC to include the software on their Alpha-contributed works CD. A bit of Linux-to-PC home networking and the discovery of the full Microsoft SMB specification gave the development effort an additional push. In

December 1993, the project resurfaced as "NetBIOS for UNIX." "Server" was temporarily recoined as "smbserver" however; the name was later discarded due to a trademark dispute with Syntax. In search of a new name for the software, Andrew looked through the UNIX /usr/dict/words database for a term that included the letters SMB. There on the screen in glowing phosphoresce was "Samba." He claims that when repeating the process now, the word seems to be missing from the database. Very spooky!

Development

The groundswell of Internet community interest in Samba required that well-known archive sites for the software be identified to provide easy access to new releases and updates. E-mail discussion lists and newsgroups were set up to provide forums for asking questions, reporting bugs, and generally kibitzing about the project (Table 4.1). Because the Samba distribution included source code, a number of porting and development efforts quickly surfaced. These ventures spanned the gamut from individual efforts to large institutional and vendor projects. Over time a core group of approximately 20 loosely knit development members surfaced that eventually became known as the *Samba Team*. As of this writing Samba has been ported to most UNIX implementations as well as to, a number of other operating systems (Table 4.2). The Samba Team is closely involved in the continuing standards work related to the SMB and CIFS specifications.

Table 4.1   *Samba Discussion Groups*

Mail Lists

samba	The Samba SMB fileserver
samba.digest	Digest form of Samba list
samba.announce	Samba announcements
samba-ntdom	NT domain controller support
samba-vms	Samba for VMS
samba-cvs	Samba CVS commit messages
samba-docs	Discussion about Samba documentation

continued on next page

Table 4.1   *continued*

samba-binaries	Developer discussions about Samba binary distributions
samba-technical	Developer discussions about Samba internals
mirrors	Samba mirror sites

To subscribe to a list e-mail: **listproc@samba.org** with "subscribe *listname* Your Full Name" in the message body. For additional information see **http://lists.samba.org/**.

Newsgroups

comp.protocols.smb	SMB protocol discussions
linux.samba	Linux Samba issues

Table 4.2   *Samba Platforms*

Servers	Non-Microsoft clients
Amiga	DAVE
HP MPE/iX	Linux SMBFS
MVS	QNX
OS/2	SCO
Stratus-VOS	Sharity
UNIX	
VMS	

Licensing

Samba is an *open source* software suite available to anyone for use under the *GNU General Public License (GPL)*. Basically this means that Samba source code will always be available and that anyone is free to modify and develop the code base as long as any derivative works are also made available per the specifications laid out in the GNU GPL. It might be helpful to take a closer look at what it means to be open-source branded and GNU GPL compliant.

Open Source Initiative

The *Open Source Initiative (OSI)* represents the next level in the evolution of grassroots, open software organizations. Like its predecessors, OSI sprang up from the collective conscience of an Internet community of users whose firm belief is that the lifeblood of the Internet is the open sharing of ideas and software. An OSI branding indicates a commitment by the technology provider that it, too, adheres to these same ideals by providing source code and specifications and encourages further development of the technology by the community at large.

The idea for an open-source branding emerged from a meeting of a few like-minded champions of a *gospel of open technology*, in February 1998 (see **http://www.opensource.org/history.html**). Participants included Todd Anderson, Chris Peterson (Foresight Institute), John Hall and Larry Augustin (Linux International), Sam Ockman (Silicon Valley Linux Users Group), and Eric S. Raymond. The catalyst for the discussion was the recent announcement by Netscape that it would make the source code to its browser available free of charge. The intent of the meeting was to set specifications that characterized an open technology, and to find a suitable name for this initiative. Chris Peterson proposed *Open Source* as an appropriate cognomen for the project. The *Debian Free Software Guidelines* also known as the *Debian Social Contract* was chosen as a basis for the *Open Source Definition* of certification (Table 4.3). Bruce Perens and Eric S. Raymond launched the OSI Website, Linus Torvalds, father of Linux, gave the initiative his blessing, and, OSI began showing up in the press and vendor product announcements, not to mention in documents like the infamous *Microsoft Halloween Document*.

Table 4.3   *OSI certification*

Free Redistribution Rights
Available Source Code
Allow Derived Works
Preservation of Integrity of Authors' Source Code

continued on next page

Table 4.3   *continued*

No Discrimination Against Persons or Groups
No Discrimination Against Fields of Endeavor
Distribution of License
License Must Not Be Specific to a Product
License Must Not Contaminate Other Software
* See OSI Web site for full details.

Software products can be OSI-certified by following the procedures described on the Web sites (listed below). Well-known products branded by the OSI include Linux, Apache, sendmail, BIND, and perl. The OSI also maintains a list of other open or free source licenses that adhere to the Open Source Definition (Table 4.4).

- Open Software Initiative
- osi@opensource.org
- http://www.opensource.org

Table 4.4   *OSI-Approved Licenses*

GNU General Public License (GPL)
GNU Library (Lesser) Public License
BSD License
X Consortium License
Artistic License
Mozilla Public License (MPL)
QPL
libpng License
zlib License
IJG JPEG Library License
OpenLDAP Public License

GNU General Public License

The *GNU General Public License (GPL)* is an artifact of the *Free Software Foundation (FSF)* founded by Richard Stallman in 1983.

Like the Open Source Initiative, the FSF was interested in promoting collaborative development within the computing community by removing the obstacles imposed by proprietary software. Note that the term "free software" does not mean "without charge" but rather refers to the "freedom" to access, modify and distribute the software for further benefit to the community. The GNU project itself was directed at building a library of tools in the spirit of this philosophy. Note that *GNU* is a recursive definition that stands for *GNUs Not UNIX*. The GPL requires that software distributed under the license must always include source code, allow for derivative works and modifications, and guarantee that any subsequent developer may also distribute the software. Any deviate of a GPL product must also follow GPL specifications. Developers may charge a distribution fee for GPL products. For the full GPL specification, visit the FSF Web page listed below.

Free Software Foundation, Inc.
59 Temple Place—Suite 330
Boston, MA 02111, USA
http://www.fsf.org
gnu@gnu.org

What Samba Can Do For You

We have already talked about how Samba represents a UNIX implementation of the SMB protocol that facilitates UNIX file system and printer sharing with Windows and LAN Manager clients. What we have not yet discussed is just how tightly Samba integrates UNIX into these environments.

Samba implements Windows domain and workgroup functionality through two UNIX service daemons, nmbd and smbd. The nmbd daemon fills a dual role as NetBIOS Name Service and NetBIOS Browser Service. The smdb daemon provides the bulk of the SMB protocol implementation for sharing resource. These two daemons along, with ancillary administrative tools and client commands, provide:

- NBNS, WINS, and DNS gateway services

- Routed network browser service
- Authentication and authorization gateway between UNIX and Windows domains
- CIFS-compliant UNIX file sharing in Windows and LAN Manager networks
- Unicode character sets and name mapping
- Opportunistic locking visible to network file system services
- UNIX printer sharing in Windows and LAN Manager networks, including automated driver installation for Windows 9x clients
- UNIX access to Windows file systems
- UNIX acting as a full domain client
- UNIX acting as a minimal primary domain controller.

Future

The Samba Team is actively improving and refining the Samba code base, whose quality has recently been substantiated by a series of benchmarks performed by *Sm@rt Reseller* in January and April 1999. System test staff at *Sm@rt Reseller* ran the Ziff-Davis NetBench benchmark against Samba 2.0 running on Red Hat Linux 5.2 and on Pacific Hitech TurboLinux 3.0.1. The results were compared against Windows NT 4.0 and Novell NetWare 5.0 running on similar hardware. In both tests, the Samba/Linux combination outperformed NT and NetWare. Samba 2.0 running on an SGI Origen 200 has also been shown to outperform the custom network storage architecture implemented in the Network Appliance F760.

Windows 2000 likely represents the most immediate challenge for the Samba Team. New features in Windows 2000 like LDAP-based Active Directory services, Kerberos 5.0 authentication, Dynamic DNS, and file system modifications are dramatic departures from the legacy SMB NetBIOS architecture. Windows 2000 will provide backward compatibility for NTLM-style operations, thus ensuring interoperability with older Windows and LAN Manager clients and servers. Technologies like Kerberos and LDAP are already widely used in the UNIX community and there are subtle differences in the way that they are implemented in Windows

2000. There is certainly an opportunity here for Samba to continue playing a role in tightly integrating both the old and new UNIX and Windows worlds. In the remaining chapters on Samba installation and configuration, we will take a closer look at issues regarding Samba and Windows 2000 coexistence.

Summary

- Samba is a UNIX implementation of the SMB protocol for sharing UNIX files and printers in Windows and LAN Manager-based networks.
- Samba was created by Andrew Tridgell of Australian National University by reverse engineering the SMB protocol.
- Samba development is a collaborative process whose primary contributors are known as the *Samba Team*.
- Samba is an "open source" software suite available to anyone for use under the *GNU General Public License (GPL)*.
- The bulk of Samba functionality is provided by the `nmbd` and `smbd` daemons.
- Samba provides NBNS, WINS, and DNS gateway services.
- Samba provides NetBIOS Browser services for single subnet and routed networks.
- Samba implements the full NT domain client protocol.
- Samba can emulate the basic functionality of an NT primary domain controller.

Part 02

Installation

Samba Installation

The time has come, the Walrus said, to cease this talk of the many Samba-related things and get right to the point of the matter. Time to roll up our sleeves and install Samba.

Install or Upgrade

The first task is to determine whether this will be a new installation or an upgrade to an existing Samba environment. If this is a new install, then go ahead and skip to the next section on Samba distribution. If you're taking the upgrade route, begin by determining the software version of your running Samba service. You may be able to verify the version number quickly by referring to the distribution directory used initially to install the software. Usually the directory name will indicate the version and release numbers. If it does not, then check the whatsnew.txt file in the top level of the distribution tree. If there is any question whether the running system corresponds to what you *believe* to be the distribution source, validate the version of the running system by invoking either the smbstatus or the smbclient command (Example 5.1).

Example 5.1   *smbstatus and smbclient version display*

```
$ smbstatus -d
Samba version 2.0.5a
Service      uid      gid      pid      machine
- - - - - - - - - - - - - - - - - - - - - - - - - - - - - - - - - - - - - - - -
No locked files
Share mode memory usage (bytes):
1048464(99%) free + 56(0%) used + 56(0%) overhead =
            1048576(100%) total
$ smbclient -L localhost
...
password:
Domain=[EYRIE] OS=[Unix] Server=[Samba 2.0.5a]
...
```

The version number will allow you to gauge differences between your current Samba environment and the new features and modifications available in the latest release. In most cases you will want to upgrade to the latest and greatest version of Samba. This will put you in the best position regarding support and problem fixes. Some sites may prefer to lag a release or two behind the current version, not wanting to be too near the bleeding edge. There might also be operating system or hardware dependencies that mandate remaining at an older release.

Next make note of any local customizations or changes that differ from the default Samba distribution. Examples include alternate directory paths for commands, libraries, and log files, and any modifications or patches to the source code. Save a copy of the Samba configuration file, `smb.conf`, and the password file, `smbpasswd`, somewhere safe, far away from the installation process. It's always a good idea to play it safe by taking a full backup of your system before making any major changes to services or configuration. The same advice of taking a system backup also applies once the installation has been completed. This will give you a reference point should you later need to restart from a clean installation base.

Distribution

Where Can I Get the Latest Stuff?

The easiest way to obtain current releases of the software, participate in Samba discussion groups, and occasionally holler for help, is to refer to the Samba Web site at **http://samba.org** (Figure 5.1). This URL actually references a link index page of mirrored Samba Web sites (Figure 5.2). Select the mirror site that is closest to your network region to obtain the fastest access and best connectivity. If you want really fast access, you might consider becoming a mirror site. There are instructions at the bottom of the mirror index page regarding how to participate as a mirror site. If you don't have Web access or maybe you prefer doing things the old-fashioned way, Table 5.1 lists the Samba archive sites accessible via anonymous FTP.

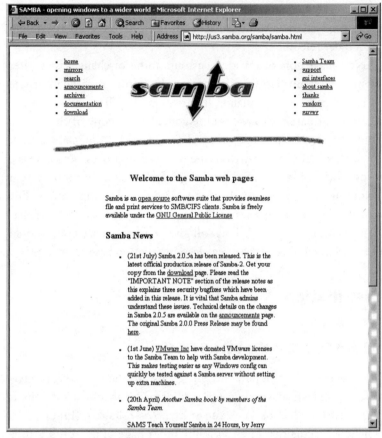

Figure 5.1   *Samba Web site*

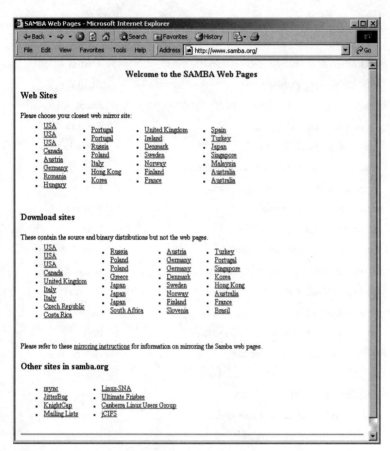

Figure 5.2   *Samba mirror index*

Table 5.1   *Samba FTP Archives*

gd.tuwien.ac.at/infosys/servers/samba/	Austria
fau1.samba.org/pub/samba/	Australia
ftp.ravel.ufrj.br/pub/unix/samba/	Brazil
ca.samba.org/pub/samba/	Canada
ftp.ucr.ac.cr/pub/Unix/samba	Costa Rica
sunsite.mff.cuni.cz/Net/Protocols/Samba/	Czech Republic
sunsite.auc.dk/pub/unix/networking/samba/	Denmark
fi.samba.org/pub/samba/	Finland
fr.samba.org/pub/samba/	France
de.samba.org/pub/mirror/samba/	Germany
ftp.uni-trier.de/pub/unix/network/samba/	Germany
ftp.ntua.gr/pub/net/samba/	Greece
it.samba.org/pub/samba/	Italy
volftp.tin.it/mirror/samba/pub/samba/	Italy
mirror.nucba.ac.jp/pub/samba/	Japan
ring.asahi-net.or.jp/pub/net/samba/	Japan
ring.aist.go.jp/pub/net/samba/	Japan
CAIR-archive.kaist.ac.kr/pub/samba/	Korea
www.bibsyst.no/pub/samba/	Norway
pl.samba.org/pub/unix/net/samba/	Poland
giswitch.sggw.waw.pl/pub/unix/samba/	Poland
pt.samba.org/pub/mirrors/samba	Portugal
ru.samba.org/pub/samba	Russia
sg.samba.org/samba/	Singapore
ftp.k2.net/mirrors/samba/	Slovenia
ftp.vwv.com/pub/samba	South Africa
se.samba.org/pub/samba/	Sweden
tr.samba.org/samba/	Turkey
sunsite.org.uk/packages/samba/	United Kingdom
ftp.samba.org/pub/samba/	USA
us1.samba.org/samba/ftp/	USA
us3.samba.org/pub/mirrors/samba.anu.edu.au/	USA

From the Samba mirror index page you can select either a *Web site* or a *download site*. The Web sites provide full access to the Samba software archives, support information, mail list archives, and newsgroups (Figure 5.3). The download sites are FTP indices of Samba software distribution and documentation directory trees (Table 5.2).

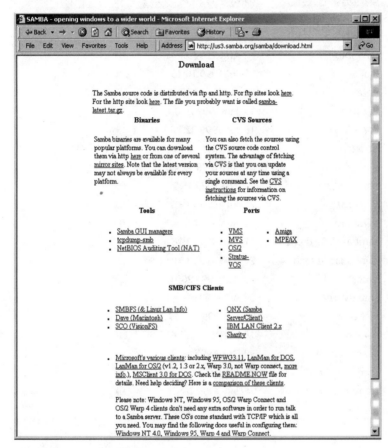

Figure 5.3   *Samba Web download page*

Table 5.2 *Samba FTP Archive*

Name	Last modified	Size	Description
Parent Directory	27-Apr-1999 02:02	0k	
Binary_Packages/	15-Jan-1999 23:03	0k	
COPYING	03-May-1996 20:38	18k	
DOWNLOADING	27-Oct-1998 22:33	1k	
MIRRORS.txt	15-Nov-1998 23:33	1k	
SMB-info/	18-Aug-1997 21:41	0k	
alpha/	19-Jul-1999 10:36	0k	
beta/	30-Dec-1998 19:53	0k	
bin-pkgs/	15-Jan-1999 23:03	0k	
contributed/	16-Jul-1999 02:17	0k	
docs/	20-Jul-1999 20:39	0k	
pam_ntdom/	01-Jun-1998 12:42	0k	
pam_smb/	22-Apr-1999 15:59	0k	
patches/	21-Jul-1999 21:16	0k	
pwdump/	18-Aug-1997 21:41	0k	
samba-2.0.5a.tar.gz	21-Jul-1999 21:16	2.1M	
samba-latest.tar.gz	21-Jul-1999 21:16	2.1M	
slides/	18-Apr-1999 20:16	0k	
smb2www/	04-Aug-1998 14:03	0k	
smbedit/	20-Jun-1999 15:17	0k	
smblib/	18-Aug-1997 21:41	0k	
snapshot/	30-Dec-1997 09:53	0k	
tcpdump-smb/	23-Jul-1999 10:57	0k	
translations/	25-Jan-1999 18:14	0k	
xfertest/	12-Dec-1998 18:57	0k	

Binary or Source

Once you have navigated to an archive site, you need to decide
whether to download a binary or source code distribution.
Precompiled packages are available for a number of popular operating systems including AIX, BSDI, Digital UNIX, Linux, SCO,

Solaris, and many others. The binary distributions can save time and trouble for those who don't want to roll their own Samba configuration. If you like that warm and fuzzy feeling you get from compiling your own software, then select the source distribution. You'll want source if you're interested in playing with the latest alpha and beta releases. Building Samba from a source distribution is very easy with the GNU `autoconf` available in version 2.x. There is more about `autoconf` later in the chapter.

Note that if you are building a Samba version prior to 1.9.81 and need to support SAM-encrypted password authentication for Windows 9x and Windows NT, you will need to obtain a copy of the `libdes` library. `libdes` is used in older versions of Samba to enable DES (Data Encryption Standard) encrypted passwords. DES technology was derived from work done by IBM in the early 1970s. Distribution of DES algorithms is governed in the United States by the International Traffic and Arms Regulations (ITAR). The good news is that as of version 1.9.18, Samba contains a modified DES algorithm that can be distributed without violating ITAR or raising the hackles of the U.S. National Security Agency.

CVS

Another reason for choosing a source code distribution is the ability to add your own modifications. One of the most common modifications is integrating Samba with unsupported authentication and authorization mechanisms. If you need to modify the source code, consider using *GNU Concurrent Versions System (CVS)*. CVS is a multiuser source code control system that allows developers to check out snapshots of source code and concurrently integrate their modifications into the source tree. Using CVS makes it easy for you to reapply local modifications into new releases of Samba. Read-only CVS access to the Samba source tree is available via the Web at **http://samba.org/cgi-bin/cvsweb/** (Figure 5.4). The CVS client software and CVS information can be obtained from **http://download.cyclic.com.**

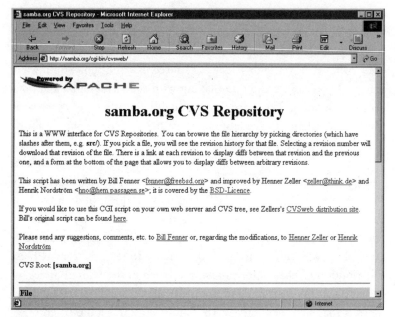

Figure 5.4   *Samba CVS site*

Versions

The current production release of Samba is packaged as `samba-latest.tar.gz`. The package contains everything you need to install and support Samba. Other distributions are labeled with the version number and a suffix indicating the patch level or whether the distribution is an alpha or beta release.

samba-latest.tar.gz	Current Production Version
samba-<*version*>.tar.gz	Other Versions

The package is in compressed tar format. Move the package into your source code maintenance directory or a temporary directory and extract it using GNU zip piped into the tar command. The expanded directory tree will look something like Example 5.2.

Example 5.2   *Extracting the Samba Distribution*

```
$ gzip -dc samba-<version>.tar.gz | tar -xvf -
$ ls -al
-rw-r--r--  1 root   system  18321  May 04  1996     COPYING
-rw-r--r--  1 root   system  3406   Nov 23  1998     Manifest
-rw-r--r--  1 root   system  6753   Jul 20  18:23    README
-rw-r--r--  1 root   system  2453   Feb 25  1999     README-smbmount
-rw-r--r--  1 root   system  1936   May 14  19:03    Roadmap
-rw-r--r--  1 root   system  19982  Jul 21  19:06    WHATSNEW.txt
drwxr-xr-x  1 root   system  0      Aug 30  08:51    docs
drwxr-xr-x  1 root   system  0      Aug 30  08:50    examples
drwxr-xr-x  1 root   system  0      Aug 30  08:50    packaging
drwxr-xr-x  1 root   system  0      Aug 30  08:50    source
drwxr-xr-x  1 root   system  0      Aug 30  08:50    swat
```

Building Samba

Compiling and installing Samba is a simple, automated process conducted using the UNIX `make` command. Version 2.x further simplifies the task by including GNU `autoconf` to tailor `Makefile` parameters to match operating system type and configuration. Pre-version 2 distributions require a bit of administrative housekeeping in that `Makefile` parameters must be set by hand. Parameters include compiler flags, install paths, and authentication methods. The `Makefile` is well documented and includes examples of common settings for most operating systems. See Table 5.3 for a listing of some of the common variables and flags. To build and install Samba, move to the top-level source distribution directory and follow the steps listed in Example 5.3.

Example 5.3   *Samba Build Process*

```
1. $ configure      Version 2.x and newer only.
2. $ make           Compile and load step.
3. $ make install   Install binaries in target directories.
```

If you are upgrading from a previous release and are using the same source distribution directory, the old release binaries are copied into a .old directory. You can recover the previous release by invoking make revert. Note that if you execute make install twice, the old release binaries will be overwritten.

$ make revert   Restore old release binaries.

Table 5.3   *Sampling of Pre-Version 2.0 Makefile Variables*

OS Flags (see Makefile)

```
FLAGSM = -D<OS Type> -DSHADOW_PWD          Shadow Passwords
LIBSM = -lshadow
CC = gcc                                   C Compiler
INSTALLPERMS = 0755                        Permissions
```

Install Directories

```
BASEDIR =/usr/local/samba
BINDIR = $(BASEDIR)/bin                     Binaries
SBINDIR = $(BASEDIR)/bin                    Binaries
LIBDIR = $(BASEDIR)/lib                     Libraries
VARDIR = $(BASEDIR)/var                     Spool dir
MANDIR = $(BASEDIR)/man                     Man pages
```

Logs & Locks

```
SMBLOGFILE = $(VARDIR)/log.smb              smbd log file
NMBLOGFILE = $(VARDIR)/log.nmb              nmbd log file
LOCKDIR = $(VARDIR)/locks                   Lock files
```

Samba Configuration Files

```
CONFIGFILE = $(LIBDIR)/smb.conf             Samba config file
LMHOSTSFILE = $(LIBDIR)/lmhosts             LMHOSTS file
DRIVERFILE = $(LIBDIR)/printers.def         W95 print drivers
SMB_PASSWD = $(BINDIR)/smbpasswd            Password utility
SMB_PASSWD_FILE =                           Password file
   $(BASEDIR)/private/smbpasswd
WORKGROUP = <Workgroup Name>                Workgroup
WEBROOT = $(BASEDIR)
```

Alternate Authentication Methods

```
PAM_FLAGS = -DUSE_PAM                        PAM
```

continued on next page

Table 5.3 *continued*

```
PAM_LIBS = -ldl -lpam

AFS_BASE = /usr/afsws                    AFS
AFS_FLAGS = -DAFS_AUTH -I$(AFS_BASE)/include
AFS_LIBDIR = $(AFS_BASE)/lib
AFS_LIBS = -L$(AFS_LIBDIR) -L$(AFS_LIBDIR)/afs \
      -lkauth -lprot -lubik -lauth -lrxkad -lsys \
      -ldes -lrx -llwp -lcom_err \
      $(AFS_LIBDIR)/afs/util.a

DCE_BASE = /opt/dcelocal                 DCE
DCE_FLAGS = -DDFS_AUTH -I$(DCE_BASE)/include
DCE_LIBDIR = -L$(DCE_BASE)/lib
DCE_LIBS =

KRB5_BASE = /usr/local/krb5              Kerberos V5
KRB5_FLAGS = -DKRB5_AUTH -I$(KRB5_BASE)/include
KRB5_LIBS = -L$(KRB5_BASE)/lib -ldes425 \
      -lkrb5 -lcrypto -lcom_err
```

Completing the Installation

When you have completed the install procedure, the Samba component tree will look something like Table 5.4. Before you can start
Samba and verify the installation you will need to install the Samba
configuration file `smb.conf`. This file indicates server role, access
controls, what shares are available, whether encrypted passwords are
required, and general administrative limits. If this is a new Samba
installation, you can copy the default `smb.conf` file from the
`./examples` subdirectory in the source distribution into the
`/usr/local/samba/lib` directory. This will allow you to start and
verify the new installation. We'll cover the details of `smb.conf` in
the next chapter.

Table 5.4   *Sampling of Samba Component Tree*

```
/usr/local/samba                        Default install tree.
    ./bin:                              Commands.
            addtosmbpass
            convert_smbpasswd
            make_printerdef
            make_smbcodepage
            nmbd
            nmblookup
            rpcclient
            smbclient
            smbd
            smbpasswd
            smbstatus
            smbtar
            swat
            testparm
            testprns

    ./lib:
            ./codepages                 Codepage directory.
            smb.conf                    Samba Configuration.

    ./man:                              Man pages.

    ./private:                          SID and passwords.
            MACHINE.SID
            smbpasswd

    ./swat:                             Swat support.
        ./help
        ./images
        ./include

    ./var:                              Logs and lock dir.
        ./locks
        log.nmb
        log.smb

    ./var/locks:                        Lock and PID files.
            STATUS..LCK
            browse.dat
            namelist.debug
            nmbd.pid
            smbd.pid
```

Operation

At this point, we've completed the installation and must now decide how we want to run the service. The two Samba service daemons, smbd and nmbd, may either be started as running daemons at system boot time or be invoked when needed by inetd. The latter method will conserve system resources in environments where Samba services are lightly used. For high-demand environments, it may be faster to have the services already up and running when they are required.

To start Samba services as always-active daemons at system boot time, add the stanzas listed in Example 5.4 to your /etc/rc.local startup script for BSD UNIX installations or as part of your /etc/rc.d/init.d functions under SYSV UNIX. The commands can also be entered from the command line as root for testing.

Example 5.4 *Samba Daemon Startup*

```
/usr/local/samba/bin/smbd -D
/usr/local/samba/bin/nmbd -D
```

To invoke Samba services under inetd, first add the service ports to /etc/services (Example 5.5). Then add the startup stanzas to /etc/inetd.conf (Example 5.5). Note the use of tcpwrappers /usr/sbin/tcpd parameter. It is a good idea to restrict access to the service using a tool like tcpwrappers. Remember that you will have to send a HUP signal to the inetd process to activate these changes in the running system.

Example 5.5 *Samba inetd Startup*

/etc/services

```
netbios-ns     137/udp
netbios-ssn    139/tcp
```

/etc/inetd.conf

```
netbios-ssn stream tcp nowait root /usr/sbin/tcpd
             /usr/local/samba/bin/smbd smbd
```

continued on next page

Example 5.5 *continued*

```
netbios-ns dgram udp wait root /usr/sbin/tcpd
               /usr/local/samba/bin/nmbd nmbd
```

With the Samba smbd and nmbd daemons running, you can verify the services using the nmblookup and smbclient commands. Use nmblookup to query the nmbd name service. You can use your local hostname as an argument. Nbmd should respond with your IP address and hostname (Example 5.6).

Example 5.6 *Samba Name Service Test*

```
$ nmblookup wizard
192.168.0.26   wizard
```

Next use smbclient to access your home directory (Example 5.7). You will be prompted for your password. If you have problems getting smbd to accept your password, check the password encryption options defined in smb.conf (Chapter 7).

Example 5.7 *Samba Shares Access Test*

```
$ smbclient //wizard/deroest
Password:
Domain = [EYRIE] OS = [Unix] Serve r= [Samba 2.0.5a]
Smb: \>
```

Summary

- If you are upgrading from a previous release, verify your version using the smbstatus or smbclient commands and back up your current environment.
- Download Samba distributions from the Samba Web site at **http://samba.org**.
- Verify the distribution version from the package file name, samba-<version>.tar.gz. A version of "latest" indicates the current production release.

- Decide whether to use a binary or source distribution.
- If you will be making local modifications to the source, consider using the GNU Concurrent Versions System (CVS). Refer to **http://samba.org/cgi-bin/cvs-web** for read-only Web-based access to Samba CVS distributions.
- Extract the distribution package in your source maintenance directory:

```
$ gzip -dc samba-<version>.tar.gz | tar -xvf -
```

- If you will be building a pre-version 2.x distribution, edit the Makefile to reflect your operating system configuration.
- Build and install the distribution.

```
1. $ configure      Version 2.x and newer only.
2. $ make           Compile.
3. $ make install   Install binaries.
```

- Install a copy of the Samba configuration file `smb.conf` in `/usr/local/samba/lib`. A sample `smb.conf` file can be found in the `./examples` subdirectory of the distribution tree.
- Configure Samba `smbd` and `nmbd` startup either as running daemons or under `inetd` control.
- Start the service and verify with the `nmblookup` and `smbclient` commands.

Part 03

Configuration

Samba Configuration—smb.conf

The Samba players have now been fashioned and arrayed upon this, our operating system stage. Time now to tender the libretto, directing the measure of their shares. In other words, we've completed the Samba installation process. Now it's time to direct our attention toward defining the server's role in the workgroup or domain and specify what resources it will share.

In this chapter, we will become familiar with the general structure and syntax of the Samba configuration file, smb.conf. This file directs the runtime behavior of both the smbd and nmbd daemons. In the ensuing Chapters 7 through 12, we'll scrutinize the specific sections and parameters of the Samba configuration file that affect authentication, name service, browsing, domain control, sharing files, and sharing printers. In Chapter 15 we will assess the administrative and event logging parameters that can be specified in smb.conf.

Appendix C includes a copy of the default smb.conf file that ships with the 2.0.5a release. It may be helpful to refer to this file as we review the configuration file structure and syntax. An online copy of this file can be found in the ./examples subdirectory of the Samba distribution tree. The file is well documented and can be used as a template for building your own configuration file. Refer to the smb.conf (5) manpage for additional information.

```
$ man 5 smb.conf
```

Tailoring smb.conf

The smb.conf file is a flat ASCII text file that can be modified with any text editor. The general format of the file is similar to that of Windows .INI files. Configuration information is broken down into *sections* and delineated by a section name (Table 6.1). Each section designates a service. A special *global* section defines overall system and administrative default, and the roles the server will assume in the workgroup or domain. The remaining sections in the file designate the resource *shares* the server will make available to network clients. Sets of well-defined *parameters* are used to specify the properties of each section. Note that some parameters only apply to the global section while others only apply to "shares" sections.

Table 6.1 *smb.conf Sections*

[Global]	System roles and defaults
[Homes]	Home directory shares
[Printers]	Printer shares
[Name]	User defined share

Syntax and Semantics

Each stanza in the `smb.conf` file represents either a *section* name, *parameter* = *value* pair, or *comment*. A section begins with a section name enclosed in square brackets. The section name is followed by a collection of parameters and values, one per line, which describes the section's role and attributes (Example 6.1). Section and parameter names are not case sensitive, although case is preserved for string values. Parameter arguments are either Boolean values or character strings (Table 6.2). Each line is terminated by a newline character. Continuations are indicated by a "\" character in traditional UNIX manner. Comment lines begin with either a "#" or a ";" character. White space is generally ignored except when found within a string value. Quotes are not required for strings containing white space and are ignored if discovered by the parser. White space is used to separate individual string entries in values represented as lists.

Example 6.1   *Sample smb.conf Section*

```
#
# A publicly accessible directory, read/write to all users.
#
[public]
        path = /usr/somewhere/else/public
        public = yes
        only guest = yes
        writeable = yes
        printable = no
```

Table 6.2   *smb.conf Syntax*

"#", ";"	Designates a comment
"\"	Continue on next line
"%"	Variable prefix
"[name]"	Section name
"parameter = value"	Designates a configuration option
"1/0", "yes/no", "true/false"	Boolean values

When making changes to your `smb.conf` file, use the `testparm` command to verify correctness. `testparm` will not guarantee that a particular share or service will work as you expect; rather it will validate the syntax and options you have specified for each section. If a host name or IP address is supplied as an option, it will check the access rights of the specified host.

```
$ testparm <-s configfilename> <hostname hostIP>
```

SWAT

For those more accustomed to the ease of use and error checking provided by a GUI configuration tool, Samba Version 2.x provides a Web-based configuration and administration tool aptly named the *Samba Web Administration Tool (SWAT)* (Figure 6.1). Being Web based, SWAT can be invoked from a remotely networked workstation. This is a handy capability for those administering a number of geographically disparate Samba servers or making late-night configuration changes over a dialup link from the comfort of home. SWAT provides HTML forms for the various section types represented in the `smb.conf` file (Figure 6.2). SWAT simplifies general configuration tasks and allows the system administrator to focus on the section definition of interest.

SWAT is installed by default in the `$(BASEDIR)/swat` directory as part of the general Samba build and install procedure. Before you can use SWAT, you need to add entries to `/etc/services` and `/etc/inetd.conf` identifying the port and service name to your system (Example 6.2). Don't forget to send a HUP signal to the inetd daemon after making your changes. Once SWAT has been configured into the system, you can invoke the service from your favorite Web browser by opening the following URL. SWAT will prompt you for the administrator's user name and password.

Warning: Be aware that SWAT will remove all *comments, include=, and copy= parameters when it rewrites your* `smb.conf` *file.* Make sure you keep this in mind if you are using these parameters to support multiple Samba installations from a common smb.conf template.

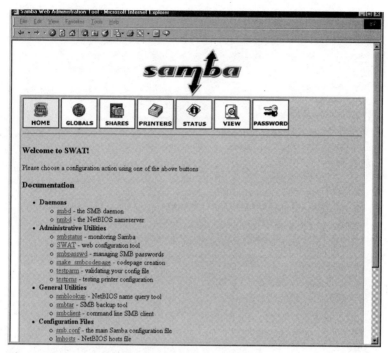

Figure 6.1   *Samba SWAT administration tool*

Example 6.2   *SWAT Internet Service Configuration*

```
/etc/services:
        swat      901/tcp
        /etc/inetd.conf:
        swat stream tcp nowait.400 root
             /usr/local/samba/bin/swat swat
```

Variable and File Substitution

A powerful Samba feature that will assist in simplifying smb.conf configuration is *variable substitution*. Samba provides a fixed set of variables, prefixed by a "%" sign, that take on values during runtime processing. Variable substitution can be used anywhere within the smb.conf file where a string value is valid. For example, the "%m" variable is often used to associate the requesting client's NetBIOS name to a local server resource like a log file.

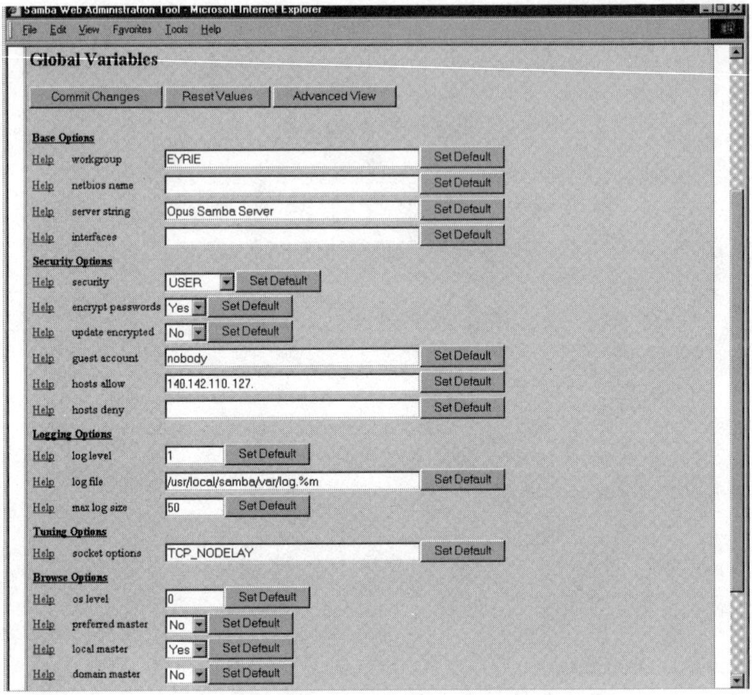

Figure 6.2   *Sample SWAT section configuration form*

```
log file = /usr/local/samba/var/%m.log
```

Given a client NetBIOS name of *WIZARD*, /usr/local/
samba/var/%m.log becomes /usr/local/samba/var/WIZARD.log.

Some variables may only be within the context of a share section.
These would include variables like the requested service name or
the validated client UNIX account name. The remaining set of variables may be used in all sections. Table 6.3 lists the set of predefined
variables in Samba Version 2.0.5a. Share section variables are listed
at the bottom of the table.

Table 6.3   *smb.conf Defined Variables*

%G = primary group name of %u

%I = the IP address of the client machine

%L = the NetBIOS name of the server. This allows you to change your config
     based on what the client calls you. Your server can have a *dual personality*.

continued on next page

%M = the internet DNS name of the client machine

%N = the name of your NIS home directory server. This is obtained from your NIS auto.map entry. If you have not compiled Samba with the auto-mount option then this value will be the same as %L.

%R = the selected protocol level after protocol negotiation. It can be one of CORE, COREPLUS, LANMAN1, LANMAN2, or NT1.

%T = the current date and time

%U = session user name (the user name that the client wanted, not necessarily the same as the one they got—i.e. UNIX user name that was actually used).

%a = the architecture of the remote machine. Only some are recognized, and those may not be 100% reliable. It currently recognizes Samba, WfWg, WinNT, and Win95. Anything else will be known as "UNKNOWN". If it gets it wrong, then sending a level 3 log to **mailto:samba-bugs@ samba.org** should allow it to be fixed.

%d = the process ID of the current server process

%h = the internet DNS hostname on which Samba is running

%m = the NetBIOS name of the client machine (very useful)

%p = the path of the service's home directory, obtained from your NIS auto.map entry. The NIS auto.map entry is split up as "%N:%p".

%v = the Samba version

Share Context Variables

%H = the home directory of the user given by %u

%P = the root directory of the current service, if any

%S = the name of the current service, if any

%g = primary group name of %u

%u = user name of the current service, if any

The `include` parameter provides another means of inserting text during `smb.conf` parsing. This parameter causes the file specified in the path value string to be inserted into `smb.conf` at the called position. If the file does not exist, the parameter is ignored. Use this facility to include machine-specific customizations when maintaining a set of Samba servers.

```
include = /usr/local/samba/lib/<server specific smb.conf text>
```

The `copy` parameter can also be used to duplicate a previously defined section at the current location. Additional parameters within the new section will override those of the previously defined share.

```
copy = <previously defined section name>
```

Runtime Automation

The `preexec` and `postexec` parameters provide a mechanism for invoking commands, shell scripts or other programs when a client accesses and releases a share respectively. The programs are executed on the server under the `%u` designated user's privileges unless the `root preexec` or `root postexec` parameters are used, which indicate that program execution will occur with root privileges. Carefully consider the application scope before using the root versions of these parameters. In most cases, alternatives can be found that produce the same results running under the calling user's privileges.

```
preexec =          <command or script path name>
postexec =         <command or script path name>
root preexec =     <command or script path name>
root postexec =    <command or script path name>
```

These parameters are useful tools for managing public resources. For example, `preexec` could be used to create and set the permissions for a personal work directory in a public lab. When the lab user disconnects from the share at logout time, `postexec` could be invoked to remove the work directory and execute other housecleaning activities like removing Web browser cookies, bookmarks, and other scratch files. Other uses for these parameters include presenting a system or informational message in a pop-up window when a share is accessed.

Global Section

The **[global]** section of the `smb.conf` configuration file describes the roles the server will play in the workgroup or domain, defines default section parameter values, and sets limits and locations for administrative files and network options. Role information includes identification of the server's NetBIOS and workgroup names and, if the server will be acting as a WINS server, a master browser or a domain controller. Section defaults provide a means for reducing the repetition of parameter values in follow-on sections. These defaults can be explicitly overridden by assigning new values in individual sections when required.

The global section is something of a catchall for Samba functions and features that aren't clearly directed at a particular resource share definition. In Chapters 7–10 and 15, we'll look closely at some of the more complex function definitions that make up the global sections. These include authentication, name service, browsing, and domain configuration. For testing purposes, you might begin with some of the general parameter definitions listed in Example 6.3. A full set of global section parameters is listed in Table 6.4.

Example 6.3 *Sample Global Section Parameters*

netbios name =	Identifies server NetBIOS name
workgroup =	Identifies workgroup or domain
guest account =	User account used for guest access to to services marked "guest ok"
security =	Specifies whether login security is set to "user," "share," "server," or "domain"
encrypt passwords =	If encrypted passwords should be negotiated for Win9x clients. Requires generation of NT encrypted passwords in the `smbpasswd` file. See `ENCRYPTION.txt` in Samba `docs` directory.
load printers =	Load browsable printer list from `printcap` file.
log file =	Samba log file directory path
max log size =	Limit log file size in kilobytes
dns proxy =	Should Samba resolve NetBIOS names via DNS lookup?

Table 6.4   *Global Parameter List*

add user script
allow trusted domains
announce as
announce version
auto services
bind interfaces only
browse list
change notify timeout
character set
client code page
coding system
config file
deadtime
debug timestamp
debuglevel
default
default service
delete user script
dfree command
dns proxy
domain admin group
domain admin users
domain controller
domain groups
domain guest group
domain guest users
domain logons
domain master
encrypt passwords
getwd cache
homedir map
hosts equiv
interfaces
keepalive
kernel oplocks

continued on next page

Table 6.4 *continued*

dap filter

ldap port

ldap root

ldap root passwd

ldap server

ldap suffix

lm announce

lm interval

load printers

local master

lock dir

lock directory

log file

log level

logon drive

logon home

logon path

logon script

lpq cache time

machine password timeout

mangled stack

map to guest

max disk size

max log size

max mux

max open files

max packet

max ttl

max wins ttl

max xmit

message command

min passwd length

min wins ttl

name resolve order

netbios aliases

netbios name

continued on next page

Table 6.4 *continued*

nis homedir

nt acl support

nt pipe support

nt smb support

null passwords

ole locking compatibility

oplock break wait time

os level

packet size

panic action

passwd chat

passwd chat debug

passwd program

password level

password server

preferred master

preferred master

preload

printcap

printcap name

printer driver file

protocol

read bmpx

read prediction

read raw

read size

remote announce

remote browse sync

restrict anonymous

root

root dir

root directory

security

server string

shared mem size

smb passwd file

continued on next page

Table 6.4 *continued*

smbrun

socket address

socket options

ssl

ssl CA certDir

ssl CA certFile

ssl ciphers

ssl client cert

ssl client key

ssl compatibility

ssl hosts

ssl hosts resign

ssl require clientcert

ssl require servercert

ssl server cert

ssl server key

ssl version

stat cache

stat cache size

strip dot

syslog

syslog only

time offset

time server

timestamp logs

unix password sync

unix realname

update encrypted

use rhosts

username level

username map

valid chars

wins proxy

wins server

wins support

workgroup

write raw

Shares Section

The *shares sections* define the explicit resources that Samba will make available to workgroup and domain clients. Two predefined sections, designated **[homes]** and **[printers]**, are provided to grant users access to their UNIX $HOME directories, and any printers listed in the UNIX printcap file. Other shares can be defined to grant or restrict access to individual directories and printers, or to specify a location for storing roaming profiles. The full set of share section parameters is listed in Table 6.5. See the smb.conf (5) manpage for a description of each parameter.

If a **[homes]** section is defined in smb.conf, it becomes the default target when no match is found for a requested share name. The share name is then assumed to be a valid user account on the server. The password file is scanned for a new match. If the user name is found, the supplied password is verified against the user's entry in the server's password file. Once validated, a new share name is created by cloning the default parameters specified in the [homes] section and associated with the user's $HOME directory. See Chapter 11 for additional information on sharing directories.

If a **[printers]** section is defined in the Samba configuration file, the server attempts to match the requested share name against the set of printers listed in the printcap file. If a match is found, a new share is created by cloning the [printers] section parameters. Refer to Chapter 12 for details on defining and sharing printers.

Table 6.5   *Share Parameter List*

admin users
allow hosts
alternate permissions
available
blocking locks
browsable
browseable
case sensitive
casesignames

continued on next page

Table 6.5 *continued*

comment

copy

create mask

create mode

default case

delete readonly

delete veto files

deny hosts

directory

directory mask

directory mode

directory security mask

dont descend

dos filetime resolution

dos filetimes

exec

fake directory create times

fake oplocks

follow symlinks

force create mode

force directory mode

force directory security mode

force group

force security mode

force user

fstype

group

guest account

guest ok

guest only

hide dot files

hide files

hosts allow

hosts deny

include

invalid users

continued on next page

Table 6.5   *continued*

level2 oplocks

locking

lppause command

lpq command

lpresume command

lprm command

magic output

magic script

mangle case

mangle locks

mangled map

mangled names

mangling char

map archive

map hidden

map system

max connections

min print space

only guest

only user

oplocks

oplock contention limit

path

postexec

postscript

preexec

preserve case

print command

print ok

printable

printer

printer driver

printer driver location

printer name

printing

public

continued on next page

Table 6.5 *continued*

queuepause command

queueresume command

read list

read only

revalidate

root postexec

root preexec

security mask

set directory

share modes

short preserve case

status

strict locking

strict sync

sync always

user

username

users

valid users

veto files

veto oplock files

volume

wide links

writable

write list

write ok

writeable

Security and Access Control

In the following chapters, we'll investigate the specific access controls and defenses on hand for hardening security and access rights to Samba shares and services. In preparation, it will be helpful to take a brief overview of some of the general access management parameters and facilities provided by Samba. As the saying goes, "An ounce of prevention is worth a pound of cure."

The first step in securing your resources is to welcome your friends and deny your enemies. Use the hosts allow and hosts deny parameters in the global and share sections to restrict access to those hosts that are trusted members of your workgroup or domain. You can specify computers by name, IP number, or by using a subnet mask. The except keyword can be used in conjunction with a subnet mask or IP number wild card to exclude individual or groups of machines (Example 6.4).

Example 6.4   *Restricting Access by Host Name or Host IP Address*

```
hosts allow = 192.168. except 192.168.0.10
hosts deny = frodo, bilbo
hosts allow = 149.125.10.0/255.255.255.0
```

You may also restrict access to an individual or a group of users using the username, only user, valid users, and invalid users parameters (Example 6.5). Depending on the parameter used, the client-supplied user name and/or password is checked against the list of user names before granting access. If the user name is prefixed with an "@" sign or a "&" sign it is assumed to correspond to an NIS netgroup. If prefixed with a "+" sign, the name is checked against the UNIX group file.

Example 6.5   *Restricting Access by User Name*

```
invalid users = root system +wheel
only user = fred
```

Sometimes you will want to make shares available to anyone. This is accomplished by specifying guest ok or only guest parameter in the share section definition. Note that even though you are granting public access to a resource, you will still want to restrict rights by mapping guest access to a known UNIX user name by using the guest account parameter (Example 6.6). This way guest rights are governed by the privileges owned by the specified account name.

Example 6.6   *Restricting Guest Access*

```
guest ok = true
guest account = nobody
```

Additional access controls may be specified for each share using the parameters listed in Table 6.6. In general, the following rules are applied when a client requests access to a share or service. Access is granted if:

- An unrestricted client passes a user name and password that maps to a permitted UNIX account name.
- A client previously registered a user name with the server and follows up by supplying a valid password.
- The client's NetBIOS name and previously used user name are checked against the supplied password.
- A client has a previously validated user name/password pair and supplies a validation token to the server.
- The share is configured with `user list` parameter and the client supplies a valid password for one of the user names in the list.
- A share is configured with a `guest account` parameter and the client supplies the valid guest account name.

Table 6.6   *Additional Access Control Parameters*

read only	Read only access
read list	
writeable	Write access ok
write ok	
write list	
printable	May print to resource
print ok	
revalidate	Revalidate on each access
group enforce named group rights	
force group	

continued on next page

Table 6.6   *continued*

force security mode	Specify permissions and umask
force directory security mode	
create mask	
security mask	
force security mask	
veto files	Hide specified files
hide files	
hide dot files	

Summary

- `smb.conf` is broken down into *global* and *share* sections.
- *Sections* are delimited by a section name enclosed in square brackets.
- Section attributes are specified from a set of predefined *parameters*.
- Parameters are represented as *parameter = value* pairs. Values are either text strings or boolean values.
- *Substitution variables* may be used to assign parameter values at runtime.
- The `include` and `copy` parameters can be used to insert or clone sections in the configuration file.
- The `preexec` and `postexec` parameters can be used to invoke commands or scripts when a client connects and releases a share respectively.
- Modifications to the `smb.conf` file can be validated using the `testparm` command.
- SWAT is a Web-based `smb.conf` configuration tool that can be used from remote workstations.
- SWAT service and port information must be defined `/etc/services` and `/etc/inetd.conf`.
- The **[global]** section defines the server's roles in the workgroup or domain, section defaults, and administrative limits.

- Share sections describe individual services and associated access rights.
- There are two predefined share sections: **[homes]** and **[printers]**.
- **[homes]** section permits connection to $HOME directories by providing the owning user name as the requested share.
- **[printers]** section permits access to printers defined in printcap file.
- Share access rights can be applied at the host, user and UNIX permission levels.

Samba Authentication

"He that has eyes to see and ears to hear may convince himself that no mortal can keep a secret. If his lips are silent, he chatters with his fingertips, betrayal oozes out of him at every pore."

Sigmund Freud

The same might be said of computer and network security. Can your server keep a secret? Do clear text passwords ooze from every network wire? In this chapter, we're going to explore various Samba authentication and access control mechanisms. We'll look at how Samba can be used to integrate and synchronize UNIX and Windows account information, interact with alternative authentication services, and reduce the use of clear-text passwords on the network.

Authentication Mechanisms

Samba supports four basic ways to regulate a network client's access rights to a particular resource share. First, Samba can allow or deny connection requests based on the client's IP address. This provides a coarse level of security. Any user with an account on a client computer that has an authorized IP address will be permitted to access the share. Second, Samba can check the client's proffered clear-text username and/or password against a UNIX authentication resource like /etc/passwd, NIS, or Kerberos. Clear-text passwords are encrypted by Samba using the associated UNIX cipher before verifying the credentials against the authentication resource. Third, Samba can negotiate NTLM style encryption with the client and validate the hashed password against a separate /usr/local/ samba/private/smbpasswd file. This option requires the maintenance and possibly the synchronization of both the server's UNIX passwd database and the smbpasswd database. Lastly, Samba can pass the client's credentials to a third-party authentication server for validation. The remote authentication server might be another Samba server or an NT domain controller. Once the credentials have been validated by the remote server, access is granted to the requested resource.

Authentication by IP Address

In the "Security and Access Control" section of Chapter 6, we discussed restricting access to shares by client IP address using the hosts allow and hosts deny parameters. Specify trusted or forbidden computers as parameter values by NetBIOS name, by IP address, or by using a subnet mask. The except keyword can be used in conjunction with a subnet mask or IP number wild card format to include or exclude individual machines from a group (Example 7.1).

Example 7.1   *Restricting Access by Host Name or Host IP Address*

```
hosts allow = 192.168. except 192.168.0.10
hosts deny = frodo, bilbo
hosts allow = 149.125.10.0/255.255.255.0
```

Authentication Level

The modus operandi for user-level authentication is determined by the global `security` parameter setting. Although the `security` parameter accepts one of four predefined values, *share, user, server*, and *domain*, in reality Samba only supports two levels of user authentication, *share* and *user*. The server and domain options are effectively extensions of user-level authentication. This setting dictates what credentials are required when a client attempts to connect to a shared resource. Generally, if you will be synchronizing user names and passwords between your Samba server and your client workstations, you will want to specify *user-level* security. If your client user names and passwords don't match those on the Samba server and you will be supporting older Windows for Workgroups clients, designate share-level security.

```
security = <share, user, server, domain>
```

Share level authentication dictates that clients supply a password associated with the requested resource before a connection is established. Note that there may be more than one password associated with a resource. For example, you might specify separate read-only and read-write passwords for a file share using the `read-list` and `write-list` parameters. Share level does not require a user name and thus does not require an SMB session setup step. If a user name is supplied, it is ignored. If guest access is permitted, the client submits a blank password. Share-level authentication was the default level in Samba releases prior to version 2.0 and for Windows 95 file and printer sharing (Figure 7.1). As of Samba Version 2.0 the default **security** setting is **user** for compatibility with Windows 98 and Windows NT.

```
security = share
```

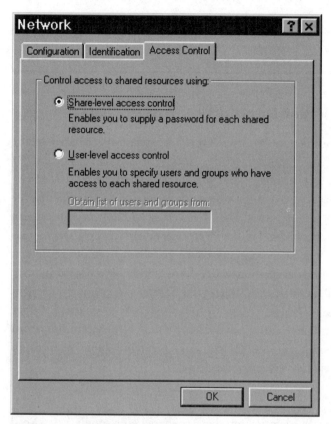

Figure 7.1   *Windows 9x security level*

User level authentication validates a client-supplied username and password against the Samba server's password database. Once it is authenticated, client access rights to the requested share are governed by the effective UID and GID permissions of the supplied username. The newly spawned **smbd** process for the connection assumes the permissions of the authenticated user name or the account permissions specified by the **admin user**, **guest account**, **force user**, and **force group** parameters. Remember that accounts identified by the **admin user** parameter are running with **root** permissions. Also note that the user name and password will be sent in the clear over the wire if the **encryption** parameter is set to no. More about this in the "Passwords" section below.

```
security = user
```

Server-level authentication is similar to user-level authentication. Samba informs the client that user-level authentication is required. The client sends a user name and password in the SMB session setup request. Samba forwards the session setup request to one of the password servers specified in the `password server` parameter. The password server returns the session UID that will be used for the connection. Note that the returned UID must either match or be mapped to a valid UID on the Samba resource servers.

```
security = server
password server = <hostname1 hostname2 ... hostnameN>
```

Domain-level authentication indicates that the Samba resource server is participating in a Windows NT domain. The client and server interactions are the same with the exception that NTLM encrypted passwords are required. The session setup request is forwarded to one of the domain controllers identified in the `password server` parameter. As with server authentication the domain user account must match or map to a valid UNIX UID. Domain-level authentication provides additional functionality in that client requests may be validated through trust relationships with other domains.

```
security = domain
encrypt = yes
password server = <pdc-name bdc1-name ... bdcN-name>
```

User Name Case

Matching user names between UNIX and Windows systems during SMB session setup isn't always as straightforward as one would hope. The problem is that even though you may maintain a consistent set of user names among all your UNIX and Windows systems, many Windows and DOS clients uppercase the user name before submitting it in a session setup request. This can be a problem if you support mixed-case usernames on the Samba server. What this means is that your Samba server has to spend CPU cycles attempting to find a match for the tendered user name by shifting the case of the letters in the string. The default behavior is that Samba will first attempt a match using all lowercase, followed by lowercase with the first letter capitalized. If the match attempt fails, then the connection request is denied. If you've got extra cycles to spare, you can request that Samba try additional combinations of upper/lower case using the `username-level` parameter. This parameter accepts a numeric value that determines the number of combinations to try. The higher the number, the more combinations will be tried:

```
username level = <0-5>
```

Username Mapping

For environments with significant disparity in existing UNIX and Windows namespaces, Samba provides a means of mapping dissimilar usernames between systems. User name mapping can also be used to map multiple user names into a single user name. The many-to-one mapping simplifies file-sharing activities among group members. User name mapping is enabled by specifying the UNIX path name of a file that contains client-to-server user name assignments as a value to the `username map` global parameter:

```
username map = </path/Filename>
```

Each line in the named mapping file assigns a valid server user name as a match to one or more client user names using an "**=**" sign character (Example 7.2). A list of client user names which are members of a UNIX group can be designated on the right side of the equation using *@groupname* syntax. An "*****" character can be used as a wildcard to indicate that any user name will match. Lines in the file can be up to 1,023 characters in length. Lines beginning with an "**#**" or "**;**" characters are ignored by the parser.

Example 7.2. *Username Mapping*

```
Syntax: username = username1 username2 ... usernameN
root = Administrator
wheel = @system
!guest = *
```

Parsing of the map file includes all lines in the file. Any line that begins with an "!" character will terminate parsing if a match was made. Failing a valid match, parsing will continue until the end of the file.

Passwords

Passwords are the backbone of most UNIX and Windows computer security systems. Therefore, most of us spend a great deal of time fine-tuning and hardening the password infrastructure. This usually means regularly checking password databases for easily guessed passwords, periodically updating password rules and dictionaries, keeping clear-text passwords off the network, schooling users on proper password use, and wrestling with users over general password policy issues. For most, it's a never-ending, thankless job.

None of us wants to increase the complexity of maintaining password services or undermine the security we've worked so hard to put in place. Unfortunately, UNIX and Windows systems don't play by the same rules when it comes to passwords. First, they employ different one-way algorithms for encrypting passwords. LAN Manager servers hash the uppercased password, Windows NT4 stores an MD4 hash of a Unicode version of the password, and UNIX uses `crypt()`, a modified DES algorithm to encrypt the password with a random salt. To further complicate matters, older Windows systems present uppercased clear-text passwords during session setup. Fortunately, Samba provides a number of options for dealing with the disparity between UNIX and Windows password schemes.

Clear-Text Passwords

Assuming your network is secure from password sniffing (*whose is?*), authorizing clear text passwords at SMB session setup time is probably the simplest method for managing passwords in a mixed UNIX and Windows environment. Conversely, it is the worst method in regard to security. The password presented to Samba by the client is validated against the UNIX password file using standard UNIX authentication methods:

```
encrypt passwords = false
security = <user or share>
```

Along with the security problems associated with clear-text passwords on the wire, you might also experience problems with clients like Windows for Workgroups that may uppercase mixed-case passwords before sending them to the server. Analogous to the previous section on uppercased usernames, Samba supplies a `password-level` parameter that directs the server to try different combinations of upper- and lowercase characters if the uppercase password check fails. The parameter accepts a numeric value that indicates the number of combinations to attempt before giving up. The higher the parameter value, the more character combinations will be tried when validating the password. A value of '0' will direct the server to check all uppercase and all lowercase renditions of the password before denying access.

```
password level = <integer value>
```

Windows NT4 at service pack 3; updated versions of Windows 95; Windows 98; and Windows 2000 all negotiate encrypted passwords only at SMB session setup. To restore support for clear-text passwords either install the appropriate registry updates available in the Samba distribution `./docs` directory (Table 7.1) or edit the registry directly using `regedit` (Example 7.3).

Table 7.1   *Windows Plain Text Password Registry Update Files*

```
./samba-<version>/docs/NT4_PlainPassword.zip
./samba-<version>/docs/Win2000_PlainPassword.zip
./samba-<version>/docs/Win95_PlainPassword.zip
./samba-<version>/docs/Win98_PlainPassword.zip
```

Example 7.3   *Registry Edit for Plain Text Password Support*

Windows NT

```
Find:HKEY_LOCAL_MACHINE\system\CurrentControlSet /
              \Services\rdr\parameters
Add:    EnablePlainTextPassword, dword:00000001
```

Windows 9x

```
Find:HKEY_LOCAL_MACHINE\System\Current\ControlSet /
              \Services\VxD\VNETSUP
Rename: "New Value #1" to
              "EnablePlainTextPasword", dword:00000001
```

Encrypted Passwords

It is possible to eliminate the clear-text password option during SMB session setup by enabling NTLM encrypted password support in Samba. The feature improves overall network security by removing the possibility of password eavesdropping on the wire; however it increases the complexity of maintaining and synchronizing the UNIX and NTLM password spaces. Enabling encrypted passwords requires maintenance of an additional password file containing NTLM passwords. This must be done in conjunction with the standard UNIX password maintenance activities.

The NTLM encrypted password option is enabled by setting the `encrypt passwords` parameter to true. Before you turn on encrypted password support you need to create an instance of the Samba `smbpasswd` file that includes an entry for each of your users. Usually the easiest way to do this is by using your existing UNIX or NIS password file as input to the `mksmbpasswd.sh` shell script supplied in the Samba distribution. The procedure is described in Example 7.4.

```
encrypt passwords = <true, false>
```

Example 7.4   *Enabling Samba NTLM Encryption Support*

```
$ cat /etc/passwd | mksmbpasswd.sh > \
/usr/local/samba/private/smbpasswd
$ chown -R root.root /usr/local/samba/private/smbpasswd
$ chmod 500 /usr/local/samba/private
$ chmod 600 /usr/local/samba/private/smbpasswd
```

Update `smb.conf` parameter.

`encrypt passwords = true`.

The `smbpasswd` file is stored in the `/usr/local/samba/private` directory by default. You can indicate an alternate location by specifying the directory path as a value to the `smb passwd file` parameter:

`smb passwd file = <path>`

The format of each entry in the `smbpasswd` file is listed in Table 7.2. In general, it is similar to standard UNIX password file format. Like its UNIX counterpart it uses a ":" to delimit each field. Take special note of the two fields that contain 32 "X" characters. These two fields are placeholders for the LAN Manager and NT versions of the hashed password respectively. It is crucial that the fields initially contain 32 "X" characters if they are to be recognized by `smbd`.

Table 7.2   *smbpasswd Format*

```
username:uid:XXXXXXXXXXXXXXXXXXXXXXXXXXXXXXXX: \
XXXXXXXXXXXXXXXXXXXXXXXXXXXXXXXX:[Account type]: \
LCT-<last-change-time>:<Long name>
```

Initially, all users have password entries consisting of 32 "X" characters. This effectively denies access to the account until the password is changed by the administrator. You can allow users to change their own passwords by overwriting the first 10 "X" characters with the string `NO PASSWORD` (Example 7.5). You will also need to enable the `null passwords` parameter so that the `smbpasswd` command can connect to the `smbd` daemon without a password. *Note that this presents a security risk in that users aren't prompted for an existing password before setting the new password value.*

Example 7.5   *Allow First-Time Password Change*

---

smb.conf

```
null passwords = true
```

smbpasswd

```
deroest:1004:NO PASSWORDXXXXXXXXXXXXXXXXXXXXXXX: \
XXXXXXXXXXXXXXXXXXXXXXXXXXXXXXXXX:[U   ]: \
LCT-00000000:Jim DeRoest:/home/deroest:/usr/bin/ksh
```

---

smbpasswd Command

The `smbpasswd` command is used to set and update the two 32-byte fields in the smbpasswd file. Note that, unlike the UNIX `passwd` command, `smbpasswd` should not have `setuid root` permission for Samba releases as of version 1.9.18p4. This version of `smbpasswd` acts as a client requesting that the authoritative Samba `smbd` daemon or NT domain PDC update the password on behalf of the end-user. Like its UNIX counterpart, the `smbpasswd` command first requests the existing password and then prompts twice for the new password (Example 7.6). Users with root permissions can include the `-u` `<username>` option to set the indicated users password.

Example 7.6   *smbpasswd Command*

```
$ smbpasswd <-u username>        Add -u if root.
old password >                   Old value if not root.
New SMB password:                New value.
Repeat New SMB Password:         New value again.
```

Migrating from Clear-Text to Encrypted Passwords

For sites that started out using clear-text passwords and wish to migrate to encrypted passwords, Samba can automate this process by setting the `update encrypted` parameter.

```
security = user
encrypt passwords = no
update encrypted = yes
```

At session setup Samba validates the client's plain text password against /etc/passwd using the default UNIX authentication process. Upon successful validation, Samba then encrypts the plaintext password into the LAN Manager and NT hashed formats and stores them in the smbpasswd file. Note that the user must already have an existing entry in the smbpasswd file. Any existing password information in the smbpasswd file will be overwritten by the new password. Once the clear text to encrypted password migration process is complete, turn off the update encrypted parameter and turn on the encrypt passwords parameter:

```
encrypt passwords = yes
update encrypted = no
```

Password Synchronization

At this point, you've completed setup of Samba encrypted password support and are now maintaining two separate password files on your server, UNIX's /etc/passwd and Samba's /usr/local/samba/private/smbpasswd. You would probably prefer an automated way to keep the two files synchronized. Updates made to one password file are automatically reflected in the other. Samba can handle one side of the problem for you. By using the unix password sync, passwd program, and passwd chat parameters, smbd will update the UNIX /etc/passwd file whenever it receives an smbpasswd change (Example 7.7). Values for the UNIX passwd command and the password chat text will need to be tailored to your specific UNIX operating system. For UNIX old timers, this is similar to setting up login chat for UUCP connections. You can tailor the chat sequence using the passwd chat debug parameter. Don't leave this option turned on during normal operation as it makes passwords visible in clear text.

```
passwd chat debug = <true, false>
```

You'll need to build something similar if you want to update smbpasswd when the UNIX passwd command is invoked. This can be tricky. You may end up with an update loop between `passwd` and `smbpasswd`. If you'd rather pass on this programming exercise, Stephen Langasek has already done some of this work for you with his `pam_smbpass` module. Samba supports add-on authentication methods through a well-defined API and shared library interface known as a *Pluggable Authentication Modules (PAM)*. We'll talk more about PAM's in the section on alternate authentication methods. `pam_smbpass` allows UNIX users to authenticate against NTLM servers and will update both password files when users change their UNIX passwords. Note that this PAM will only work on the local Samba server, so it can't be used to maintain remote password files in a distributed environment. Stephen's `pam_smbpass` is available from **ftp://ftp.netexpress.net/pub/pam**.

Example 7.7 *Synchronize Samba smbpasswd and UNIX passwd Updates*

```
encrypt passwords = yes
security = user
unix password sync = yes
passwd program = /usr/bin/passwd %u
passwd chat = *password* %n\n *password* %n\n *successful*
```

You might also be interested in periodically synchronizing your NT SAM database with the `smbpasswd` file. Jeremy Alison of the Samba Team created a tool named `pwdump.exe` that will export a copy of SAM accounts into a file in `smbpasswd` format. The program must be run from the Administrator account on NT. The `pwdump.exe` tool is available from the samba distribution sites.

```
pwdump > smbpasswd
```

Domain Authentication

Rather than have Samba do the work of maintaining the password space, you can pass this task on to a remote server. The remote server is identified using the `password server` parameter. Interactions with the remote server can either be in user-level authentication or domain-level authentication modes as designated by a `security`

parameter value of server or domain respectively. Domain-level
authentication offers some additional functionality that you'll want
to consider when choosing a remote authentication method. Under
domain-level authentication, there is no need to duplicate NTLM
and UNIX accounts. The Samba server can also participate in
domain trust relationships.

To join Samba with an exiting domain, begin by stopping the smbd
and nmbd daemons on the server. Add the server's NetBIOS name to
the domain using Server Manager for Domains on the domain controller (Figure 7.2). On the Samba server, create a server account password for the domain using the smbpasswd command (Example 7.8).
The password will be stored in the /usr/local/samba/private
directory as file named <Domain Name>.<Samba Name>.mac. The
mac file name suffix stands for *machine account*. Lastly, update the
smb.conf configuration file with the parameters and values listed in
Table 7.3. The machine password timeout parameter specifies a
time value in seconds that causes smbd to periodically regenerate a new
server domain password. Restart the smbd and nmbd daemons.

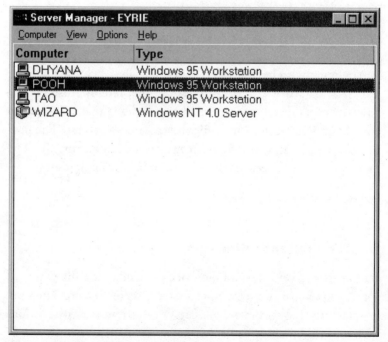

Figure 7.2   *Server manager for domains*

Example 7.8   *Creating a Domain Server Password*

```
$ smbpasswd -j <Domain Name> -r <Server NetBIOS Name>
```

Table 7.3   *smb.conf Domain Parameters*

```
security = domain
workgroup = <domain name>
password server = <PDC BDC1 ... BDCn>
encrypt passwords = true
machine password timeout = <seconds>
```

Alternative Authentication Methods

In keeping with the spirit of open-source software development, a number of alternative authentication methods have been implemented by Samba users and made available to other Samba aficionados. Some of these authentication methods are packaged as contributed tools, others have found their way back into the Samba distribution. This area of development is a moving target and thus the best source of information are the Samba discussion groups. You can also glean a fair amount of information from the smb.conf(5) man page and the distribution source code. In particular take a close look at the passdb.c and pass_check.c C-language source files located in the distribution ./source/passdb directory.

Samba-supported alternate authentication methods, databases and channels include Kerberos, Network Information Service+ (NIS+), Lightweight Directory Access Protocol (LDAP), MySQL, Distributed Computing Environment (DCE), Pluggable Authentication Module (PAM), GINAs (replaceable NT authentication modules), and Secure Sockets Layer (SSL). Of particular note is PAM functionality. PAM provides a consistent interface for implementing alternate authentication systems through the use of shared libraries and a well-defined PAM configuration table, /etc/pam.d/login. Administrators can easily change the authentication method by adding/removing libraries and updating the PAM configuration table (Example 7.9).

Example 7.9   *Sample PAM Configuration Table*

```
Service   module_type   module_path   options
login     auth          required      pam_smb _auth.so
login     auth          required      pam_kerberos.so   use_first_pass
login     auth          optional      pam_netware.so    use_mapped_pass
```

To address the issue of scaling Samba user namespace for large populations, alternative authentication databases like Kerberos, LDAP, and MySQL are under development. Kerberos 5.0 support is of particular interest in that it is base authentication method in Windows 2000. LDAP is also important, because a growing number of vendors are developing applications that use LDAP to store user validation information, including the Active Directory System in Windows 2000. Table 7.4 lists the experimental parameters available in Samba.

Table 7.4   *Global Section LDAP Parameters*

ldap server	LDAP server DNS name
ldap port	LDAP server port number
ldap root	LDAP bind entity
ldap root password	LDAP bind password
ldap suffix	LDAP distinguished name base
ldap filter	Search %u filter
SSL	

A method to further secure the SMB session channel is provided by incorporating *Secure Sockets Layer (SSL)* into Samba. SSL is technology that uses public-key encryption and X.509 digital certificates to authenticate and secure a communication channel for communication between principals. SSL is commonly used by Web applications that require secure data interchange, like electronic banking.

SSL can be added to Samba by building the distribution with *SSLeay*. SSLeay is a free implementation of the SSL protocol. A copy of SSLeay can be obtained from **ftp://ftp.psy.uq.oz.au/pub/ Crypto/SSL**. Build and install SSLeay before compiling and linking Samba. Edit the Samba `Makefile`, uncomment, and tailor the

SSL_ROOT definitions listed near the end of the Makefile definitions. Build and install Samba. There are a number of Samba SSL parameters (Table 7.5) that will need to be configured for your installation. See the smb.conf(5) man page and ./textdocs/SSLeay for details on installing, configuring and setting up certificates and keys for Samba SSL support.

Once Samba is enabled for SSL, you will need to install SSL CIFS clients on your Windows workstations. A commercial CIFS SSL client called Sharity is available from **http://www.obdev.at/ Products/Sharity.html**.

Table 7.5 *Global Section SSL Parameters*

ssl	Enable SSL.	
ssl	hosts	Force SSL for these hosts.
ssl	hosts resign	Hosts not forced into SSL mode.
ssl	CA certDir	Certificats directory.
ssl	CA certFile	Trusted certificate autorities.
ssl	server cert	Samba server certificate.
ssl	server key	Samba server private key.
ssl	client cert	Client certificate.
ssl	client key	Client private key.
ssl	require clientcert	Require client certificate.
ssl	require servercert	Require server certificate.
ssl	ciphers	SSL negotiated ciphers.
ssl	version	SSL negotiated version.
ssl	compatibility	Support other SSL implementations.

Windows 2000

As of this writing, the jury is still out regarding Samba authentication with Windows 2000 domains and forests. To ensure backward compatibility with older Windows clients and servers, Windows 2000 will support NTLM authentication in conjunction with its preferred Kerberos 5.0 and Active Directory authentication system. NTLM compatibility should allow Samba to participate in Windows 2000 domains and forests. Samba Kerberos development efforts may also allow Samba to authenticate to a Windows 2000 realm through trust relationships similar to MIT and Windows 2000 trust relationships.

Summary

- Minimum authentication requirements can be met using host-based access control using host name and/or IP address with hosts allow and hosts deny parameters.

  ```
  hosts allow = 192.168. except 192.168.0.10
  hosts deny = frodo bilbo
  ```

- Four authentication levels are supported by Samba under the security parameter, share, user, server, and domain.

  ```
  security = <share, user, server, domain>
  ```

- Share-level security only requires a valid password before granting access to a resource.
- User-level security requires a valid user name and password.
- Server-level security is like user-level security, but the user name and password are forwarded to a security server designated by the password server parameter for validation.

  ```
  security = server
  password server = My-Auth-Server
  ```

- Domain-level security is like server-level security, but Samba is participating as a full domain member and encrypted authentication is handled by a domain controller.

  ```
  security = domain
  encrypt = true
  password server = <PDC BDC1 BDC2 ... BDCn>
  ```

- Samba directs clients to supply either clear-text or encrypted passwords during session setup via the encrypt passwords parameter.

  ```
  encrypt passwords = <true, false>
  ```

- Older Windows clients may uppercase user names and passwords before submitting them during session setup. Samba can be directed to try combinations of the clear-text strings using the username level and password level parameters.

- On systems with disparate user namespaces, user names can be mapped between systems using the `username map` parameter. This parameter specifies a text file of user name mappings, one per line.
- Encrypted password support on the local Samba server requires the creation of an NTLM password file named `smbpasswd`. The file can be created from an existing UNIX password file using the supplied `mksmbpasswd.sh` script.

```
$ cat /etc/passwd | mksmbpasswd.sh > \
/usr/local/samba/private/smbpasswd
     $ chown -R root.root /usr/local/samba/private/
               smbpasswd
     $ chmod 500 /usr/local/samba/private
$ chmod 600 /usr/local/samba/private/smbpasswd
```

- NTLM passwords stored in the `smbpasswd` file are maintained by users and administrators using the `smbpasswd` command.
- Clear-text password environments can be migrated to requiring encrypted passwords using the `updated encrypted` parameter. This causes the encrypted forms of the passwords to be stored in `smbpasswd` as they are used.

```
security = user
        encrypt passwords = no
        update encrypted = yes
```

- Windows NT 4.0 with SP3 and newer Windows 9x clients default to encrypted-only support. Registry modification is required to restore clear-text password support.
- Samba can be directed to synchronize the NTLM and UNIX password files as changes are made by using the `UNIX password sync` parameter.

```
encrypt passwords = yes
security = user
unix password sync = yes
passwd program = /usr/bin/passwd %u
passwd chat = *password* %n\n *password* %n\n
             *successful*
```

- Alternate authentication methods are supported through user-contributed software. Alternate methods include Kerberos, Network Information Service+ (NIS+), Lightweight Directory Access Protocol (LDAP), MySQL, Distributed Computing Environment (DCE), Pluggable Authentication Module (PAM), GINAs (replaceable NT authentication modules), and Secure Sockets Layer (SSL).

08

Name Service

Name Service is the glue that logically "binds" a network together (pun intended for UNIX System Administrators). Name Service gives the network a methodology for registering resource names, enforcing uniqueness in the namespace, ensuring timely distribution of namespace updates, and resolving resource addresses from human readable names. Name Service can also be used to reflect the administrative structure of an organization, although this is not a requirement. Basically, Name Service simplifies finding your way around on the wires.

In its simplest form, Name Service can be implemented by using a *host table*; this is a flat ASCII text file that maps resource names and network addresses. References to a resource name are resolved to the associated network address via a simple table lookup. A copy of the host table must be distributed to each machine participating in the namespace and maintained as a set. Host tables work well for small collections of networked machines and in situations where you want to enforce a different view of the namespace on particular machines.

Larger networks require automated name service mechanisms to guarantee that namespace uniqueness remains consistent over large populations of computers. Automation is also required to ensure that namespace updates can be administered in a distributed manner and that changes are quickly reflected in all participating machines. In the Internet world, automated name service methodology is provided by the *Domain Name Service (DNS)*. Windows supports a similar NetBIOS based name service known as *Windows Internet Name Service (WINS)*.

Before diving into the details of Samba Name Service configuration, I want to stress the importance of having a firm understanding of the NetBIOS naming, registration, and query mechanisms. This background will help you better understand how the various smb.conf parameters affect Samba's role as client, server, or proxy agent. The topic of NetBIOS name service was discussed earlier in Chapter 3. I would suggest reviewing the pertinent sections of Chapter 3 before proceeding with the following sections. We'll also briefly review NetBIOS naming in the following section.

NetBIOS Names

You may recall that all NetBIOS resources are branded by a 16-byte identifier that represents the resource's unique name or group name (Example 8.1). The first 15 characters represent the alphanumeric name that identifies the resource. The 16th byte is a hexadecimal number that designates the type of resource (Table 8.1).

Example 8.1   *NetBIOS Name*

`\\<15byte_NetBIOS_name>[00h]`

Table 8.1   *NetBIOS Resource Types*

Unique Resource Type

<00>	Workstation service name
<03>	Messenger service name
<06>	RAS server
<1B>	Domain master browser
<1F>	NetDDE service
<20>	Server service
<21>	RAS client
<BE>	Network monitor agent
<BF>	Network monitor utility

Group Resource Type

<1C>	Domain group name
<1D>	Master browser name
<1E>	Group name for elections
<20>	Internet group

In the *NetBIOS over TCP/IP (NBT)* world supported by Samba, NetBIOS names are registered and resolved in one of three ways. The first and simplest method is to use a host table that manually maps NetBIOS names to IP addresses. This table is affectionately known as the *LAN Manager Hosts (LMHOSTS)* table. Each line in the LMHOSTS table matches a NetBIOS resource name to its home IP address (Example 8.2).

Example 8.2   *Sample Windows LMHOSTS Table*

```
149.110.5.12   Wizard  #PRE    #DOM:EYRIE
149.110.5.11   Dragon
149.110.5.2    Dhyana
149.110.5.1    Tao
149.110.5.5    Rose
```

The second method registers and resolves NetBIOS names using *network broadcasts* (Figure 8.1). To make its presence known, a machine broadcasts its name over the network on UDP port 137. This usually occurs at system boot time when network services are starting. The machine then awaits a response indicating whether its chosen name is accepted or rejected as being already in use by another machine (Figure 8.2). The process may be repeated a number of times, because broadcast delivery is not guaranteed. Upon successful registration, the NetBIOS name and address are cached in a collaborative manner by the workgroup of machines. NetBIOS name resolution queries are handled in a similar fashion. This method can break down quickly on large, complex networks due to routing problems and/or heavy broadcast traffic.

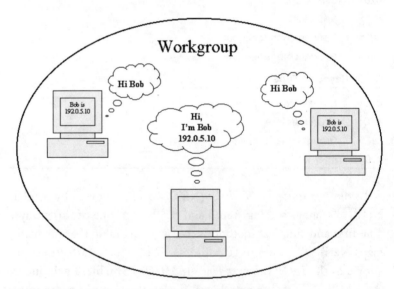

Figure 8.1   *NetBIOS broadcast name registration*

The third method for managing the namespace is similar to the preceding broadcast method, but instead of using broadcasts, it employs point-to-point communication with a designated name server (Figure 8.3). Name registration and IP address resolution requests are directed to a *NetBIOS Name Server (NBNS)* in a manner similar to Internet dynamic DNS. NetBIOS point-to-point name service protocol is defined in RFC 1001 and RFC 1002, and is implemented by

Microsoft as WINS. WINS automates the process of registering and resolving NetBIOS names, reduces NetBIOS broadcast traffic on the network and enables multi-subnet browsing. Multiple NT WINS servers can be deployed and configured to synchronize their NetBIOS data periodically to ensure availability and redundancy.

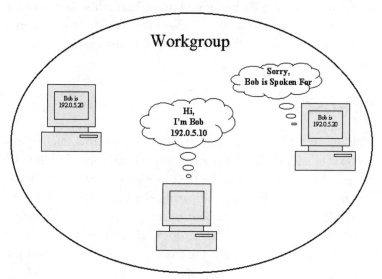

Figure 8.2   *NetBIOS broadcast name already in use*

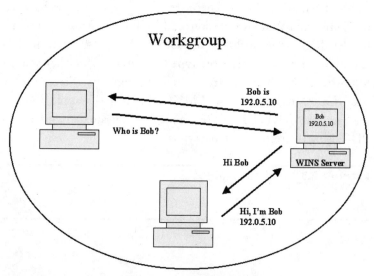

Figure 8.3   *WINS point-to-point name registration*

Samba Name Service

Now we're ready to take a close look at the various roles Samba can play regarding NetBIOS Name Service. It turns out that Samba is extremely flexible when it comes to name service options. At one extreme, Samba can be configured to use host tables to describe a simple workgroup world. At the other extreme, Samba can act as a WINS server or hybrid WINS/DNS proxy agent interacting with large Windows domains.

LMHOSTS

The easiest way to integrate Samba resources into a small work-group is by adding the Samba server to the workgroups LMHOSTS table and making a copy of the table available to the Samba **nmbd** daemon. This is done by indicating the directory path to the LMHOSTS file as an argument to the -H option when starting nmbd (Example 8.3). The default location for LMHOSTS is the same directory that contains the Samba smb.conf configuration file.

Note that LMHOSTS information is only available to the local machine. The contents are not used by Samba to resolve broadcast queries from other clients. There are also a few differences between the Samba and Windows versions of LMHOSTS. Most important-ly, NetBIOS name entries can include a suffix of a "#" character fol-lowed by a two digit resource type (Example 8.4). Other strings following a "#" character are treated as comments. The entry for host *Wizard* in the Windows LMHOSTS table (Example 8.2) and the Samba LMHOSTS table (Example 8.4) indicate that Wizard is a PDC using the respective table syntax.

Example 8.3   *nmbd and LMHOSTS*

```
nmbd -H <lmhosts path> -D
```

Example 8.4   *Sample Samba LMHOSTS Table*

149.110.5.12	Wizard#1B
149.110.5.11	Dragon
149.110.5.2	Dhyana
149.110.5.1	Tao
149.110.5.5	Rose

WINS

We've already talked about how WINS streamlines NetBIOS name service. The primary features are WINS automation of namespace maintenance due to the dynamic nature of NetBIOS name registration, the reduction in broadcast traffic through point-to-point communications between WINS client and server, and support of browsing across subnets (Figure 8.4).

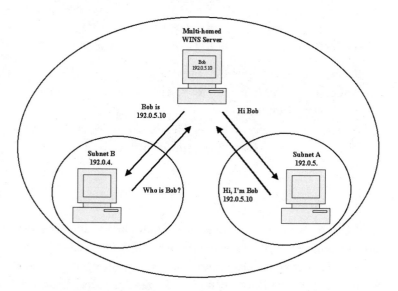

Figure 8.4   *Multi-subnet WINS*

Samba can participate in a WINS environment by assuming any one of four roles. It can act as a WINS client interacting with a designated WINS server. It can adopt the responsibility of the primary

WINS server, registering and resolving client requests. It can proxy local WINS requests to a remote WINS server. It can resolve WINS name requests against Internet DNS. This rich set of options makes Samba an exceptionally useful tool in designing complex WINS environments.

WINS Client

In order for Samba to interact seamlessly with the resources in a WINS-managed workgroup or domain, it must first register with the designated WINS server. This is accomplished by indicating the IP address or DNS name of the target WINS server as an argument to the global `wins server` parameter. Note that if the WINS server is multi-homed (multiple network interfaces), clients residing on one interface subnet will be able to browse and access Samba shares that reside on the other interface subnet:

```
wins server = <DNS name or IP address of WINS server>
```

WINS Server

Samba can also be configured to operate as a primary WINS server. Use the `wins support` parameter to enable or disable Samba as a WINS server. Note that the `wins support` and the `wins server` parameters are mutually exclusive. The former indicates that Samba is acting as a *WINS server*. The latter identifies Samba as a *WINS client*:

```
wins support = <true, false>
```

When running as a WINS server, Samba stores client registration information as ASCII text in the `wins.dat` file. The `wins.dat` database is located by default in the `./samba/var/locks` directory. Each entry includes the NetBIOS name, resource type, IP address, and broadcast address.

WINS replication is not supported by Samba. Windows NT WINS servers can replicate WINS data with each other by providing fault tolerance and load sharing in large networks. For this reason, you might want to consider using Windows NT for WINS services rather than using the Samba WINS service. If you decide to use Samba as a WINS server, remember that only one server can be deployed for a given workgroup or domain. Using more than one Samba WINS server will result in partitioning or fragmenting access to computers in the workgroup or domain.

WINS Proxy

Environments that have older Windows or LAN Manager clients that reside on multiple subnets might want to consider using Samba's WINS proxy facility. Enabling Samba's global wins proxy parameter instructs Samba nmbd to forward any broadcast name registrations or queries it receives to the designated WINS server for the workgroup or domain. Using Samba as a WINS agent allows you to leverage older clients into a WINS managed workgroup or domain:

```
wins proxy = <yes, no>
```

WINS DNS Proxy

Another Samba feature that can simplify administration of complex WINS networks is to allow nmbd to look up NetBIOS names via Internet DNS. When Samba nmbd is operating as a WINS server, and a name check against the registered WINS database fails, a second nmbd process is spawned to check the name against DNS. Note that because NetBIOS names are limited to 16 characters in length, the requested name may be truncated, and some DNS lookups may fail.

To enable Samba DNS proxy support, set both the global dns proxy and wins support parameters to true. Samba must be operating as a WINS server to resolve name queries via DNS.

```
wins support = true
dns proxy = true
```

LMHOSTS and WINS

In some instances it may be helpful to have Samba resolve its own NetBIOS name queries using both the LMHOSTS table and

WINS service. For example you might want to override WINS registrations for a particular name by setting an explicit entry in the
LMHOSTS file. Using the `name resolve order` parameter you
can instruct Samba to check LMHOSTS before trying WINS.
Note that this feature is not supported for resolving remote queries
when Samba is operating as a WINS server or proxy.

```
name resolve order = <lmhosts wins>
```

Windows 2000 Name Service

Windows 2000 departs from the WINS track in that it relies on
DNS for resolving names. The Active Directory component of
Windows 2000 uses Internet-style domain names for naming
objects in the directory. Internet domain names are translated into
domain component entries when resolving object names in the
directory (Example 8.5). WINS integration support is included in
Windows 2000 for backward compatibility with older clients and
servers. Two special DNS resource record types, **WINS** and
WINS-R, are used to designate WINS servers to be used when
resolving NetBIOS names. The WINS servers are consulted when a
local DNS lookup fails. This facility can also be used to set up a
WINS-only DNS zone for referrals using an explicit subdomain.
For example, you might define a DNS subdomain called `wins`. Any
DNS queries for domain names that include this subdomain would
be refered to the DNS server that resolves WINS NetBIOS names.
Refer to "Using WINS Lookup" in Windows 2000 help for more
information. Windows NT 4.0 WINS/DNS integration can also be
used to map WINS NetBIOS names into DNS as a transition
bridge between WINS environments and Windows 2000.

Example 8.5   *DNS to Domain Component Name*

```
DNS:    opus.cac.washington.edu
DC:     DC=opus,DC=cac,DC=Washington,DC=edu,o=Internet
```

Summary

- Workgroup and domain resources are identified by a 16-character NetBIOS name.

- NetBIOS names are registered and resolved by using host tables, collaborative broadcasts and caching, or point-to-point communication with name servers.

- The NetBIOS host table known as the LMHOSTS file represents the simplest method of mapping NetBIOS names to IP addresses.

- NetBIOS broadcasts provide an automated registration and resolving service but may result in a significant amount of broadcast traffic in large networks and may be limited by subnet.

- Windows Internet Name Service (WINS) uses point-to-point communication with designated WINS servers to register and resolve names. WINS services reduce broadcast traffic and can span subnets.

- Samba supports LMHOSTS, broadcast, WINS and hybrid WINS operation.

- LMHOSTS lookup is enabled by invoking `nmbd` with the `-H` option which identifies the directory path to the LMHOSTS file.

- To configure Samba as a *WINS client* use the `wins server` parameter to identify the WINS server by IP address or DNS name.

- To configure Samba as a *WINS server* enable the `wins support` parameter. Remember that `wins server` and `wins support` are mutually exclusive.

- Use Samba to proxy broadcasts from older Windows and LAN Manager clients to a target WINS server by enabling the `wins proxy` parameter.

- Allow Samba, when operating as a WINS server, to look up names via DNS as well as the WINS database by enabling the `dns proxy` parameter.

- Instruct Samba to resolve NetBIOS names by both LMHOSTS and WINS by specifying the order using the `name resolve order` parameter. Note that this is only used for local queries by Samba.

Browsing

In Chapter 8 we looked closely at the underpinnings of how Samba interoperates with WINS NetBIOS name service. Specifically, we learned how to configure Samba to operate as a WINS client, server or proxy agent. Now that we have the means for resolving the network address of a system from its NetBIOS name, how do we discover the full set of NetBIOS resource names that are available in a workgroup or domain?

Like vendor product advertisements in shopping catalogs, work-group and domain computers publicize their file and print shares in lists that are made available to perspective clients. This practice is known as *browsing* and is exclusive to Microsoft network architecture. A hierarchical set of *browser servers* (Table 9.1) collects and synchro-nizes the lists of shares called *browse lists*. The servers make the browse lists available to *browser clients* on request. A common browser client is the Windows Network Neighborhood client (Figure 9.1). The browsing scope of available shares is grouped by workgroup or domain. This simplifies the task of locating desired resources in large networks comprised of multiple workgroups and domains.

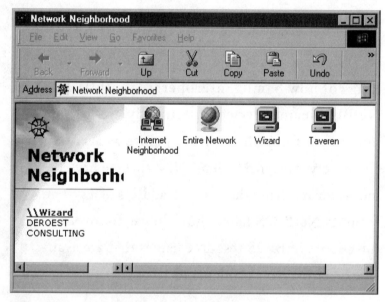

Figure 9.1   *Browsing the network neighborhood*

Table 9.1   *Browser Server Types*

Domain Master Browser   Collects browse lists for entire domain. Provides authoritative copies of the browse list to local master browser servers on each subnet. The PDC of an NT domain is automatically des-ignated the domain master browser.

continued on next page

Table 9.1   *continued*

Local Master Browser	Collects the list of servers and shares in a work-group or domain. One local master browser server is elected per subnet.
Backup Browser	Maintains a copy of the browse list obtained from a master browser and makes it available on request to workgroup or domain clients.

Elections

The list of available shares on each computer in a workgroup or domain is broadcast by the owning system out to the network community. Because the announcement is via a network broadcast, a *local master browser* server is required on each subnet to collect and collate the set of shares into a browse list. The local master browser is elected from a set of computers on the subnet that is capable of maintaining and serving browse lists. The election process is a network-bidding feud where the ante is based on the contender's OS level and revision, and its desire to be a master browser. This ante or credential is called an *election criterion* (Table 9.2). The computer with the highest election criteria becomes the local master browser for the subnet. The losers are demoted to *backup browsers* for redundancy and load sharing purposes. New elections are called on a periodic basis, at boot time, and by a client due to a communication error.

To support workgroup and domain browsing across subnets, a *domain master browser* must be designated. The domain master browser periodically collects and synchronizes the browse lists maintained by the local master browsers that reside on each subnet. The identity of the domain master browser is registered and maintained by WINS. In the case of a Windows NT domain, the PDC always acts as the domain master browser. In single subnet NT domains, the PDC is both the domain master browser and local master browser.

Each local master is considered "authoritative" for share information obtained from its own subnet. It is considered "non-authoritative" for browse lists obtained via communication with the domain master browser. The local master browsers periodically resynchronize their browse lists with the domain master browser. Note that if a network problem results in a partitioned network, bad browse list information may remain persistent for up to 36 minutes.

Table 9.2   *Election Criteria*

OS Level		
Windows for Workgroups	0x01	1
Windows NT Workstation	0x10	16
Windows NT Server	0x20	32
Desired Role		
Backup Browser	0x01	1
Standby Browser	0x02	2
Master Browser	0x04	4
Domain Master Browser	0x08	8
WINS Client	0x20	16
Windows NT Server	0x80	64

Samba and Browsing

As of release 1.9.17a, Samba has supported the full set of browser functionality including replication and synchronization of browse lists across subnets. Like Samba WINS service, Samba browsing options include hybrid features not found in native Windows implementations.

Table 9.3 lists the set of available global and service level `smb.conf` parameters that affect browser operation. After reviewing these parameters, we'll look at the specific combinations of parameters required to implement browser support in workgroups, domains, and across one or more subnets.

Table 9.3   *Samba Browser Parameters*

Base Parameters

workgroup = <*workgroup name*>	Workgroup/Domain Name.
netbios name = <*NetBIOS-Name*>	Primary NetBIOS Name.
netbios aliases = <*Alias1 ... AliasN*>	Other NetBIOS Aliases that may also be used to identify the server.
interfaces = <*IP-addr1 ... IP-addrN*>	The set of hardware interfaces used for browser communications (multi-homed).

LAN Manager Paramters

lm announce = <*true, false, auto*>	Will nmbd produce lanman announcements for OS/2 client? Required if OS/2 clients need to see browse lists. A value of "auto" indicates that it should not send them by default. Nmbd will listen and respond when needed.
lm interval = <*seconds*>	Period between lanman announcements; if '0', no announcements will be made.

Election Parameters

browse list = <*yes, no*>	Will server support browse lists?
announce as = <NT, Win95, WfW>	OS type Samba will announce.
announce version = <*version number*>	OS version Samba will announce. Default 4.2 is higher than 4.0 announced by NT.
os level = <*integer*>	OS level for election criteria; a value of '65' will exceed NT Server.
local master = <*yes, no*>	Indicates if Samba should try to become local master.
preferred master = <*yes, no*>	Indicates that Samba will force an election on startup and attempt to become a master browser. Used to weight browser election in Samba's favor.
domain master = <*yes, no*>	Samba is domain master and will collate and synchronize browse lists between local master browsers. DO NOT USE IF AN NT PDC ALREADY EXISTS FOR THE DOMAIN.

continued on next page

Table 9.3 *continued*

Share and List Parameters

auto services = <*list*>	The set of local share names you want added to the browse list
browsable = <*yes, no*>	Is this share browsable?
comment = <*text*>	Share description for browse lists
load printers = <*yes, no*>	Add all printers in the printcap file to the browse list?
server string = <*text*>	Description of the server for the browse list.

Hybrid Parameters

remote announce = <*IP-addr/WORKGROUP*>	Force propagation of local browse list to set of remote IP address announcing with alias WORKGROUP names. If WORKGROUP is omitted, then workgroup parameter value is used.
remote Browse Sync = <*IP list*>	List of remote master browsers to force browse list synchronization; this option only works with Samba local master browsers.

Browser Configuration

When configuring Samba to interoperate in a Windows and/or LAN Manager browsing environment, first delineate the NetBIOS name that will be used to identify the Samba server and its workgroup or domain name. These are specified by the netbios name and workgroup parameters in smb.conf. It should be obvious that these values are required for Samba's shares to be identified in browse lists.

```
workgroup = <workgroup name>
netbios name = <NetBIOS name>
```

Verify that the global guest account parameter is set for a valid UNIX account on the server. This is so that the IPC$ service used to list shares is run under guest account permissions.

```
guest account = <UNIX account name>
```

Samba will also need to announce itself as one of the Windows operating system types to indicate its browser functionality. This is accomplished by setting the `announce as` and `announce version` parameters to impersonate Windows for Workgroups, Windows 95, or Windows NT.

```
announce as = <NT, Win95, WfW>
announce version = <version number>
```

Now define what browser role Samba will play in the workgroup or domain by setting the `domain master`, `local master`, `preferred master`, and `os level` parameters. These parameters determine whether Samba will act as a client or a server and if the latter, how it will influence the master browser election process. At this point let's assume we are running within a workgroup on a single subnet or flat network.

Browser Client

First, we'll assume that Samba should announce its shares but will not maintain browse lists (Figure 9.2). Let somebody else do the work of the local master and backup browsers. Disable the domain master, local master, and preferred master parameters. Set the `os level` to zero. This configuration will inhibit Samba from becoming a master browser:

```
domain master = no
local master = no
preferred master = no
os level = 0
```

Local Master Browser

If you would like Samba to do its share of the work and maintain and serve browse lists as a master or backup browser (Figure 9.3), then enable the `browse lists` and `local master` parameters. The `preferred master` parameter will help Samba edge out contenders if there is a tie in `os level` values. The `browse lists` parameter indicates that Samba will serve lists when it receives a `NetServerEnum` call.

```
domain master = no
  local master = yes
  preferred master = yes
  os level = 65
  browse lists = yes
```

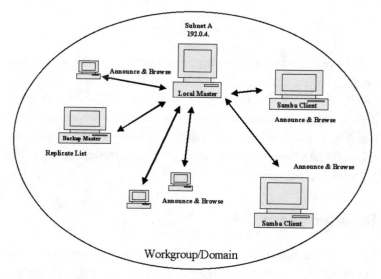

Figure 9.2   *Samba as a browser client*

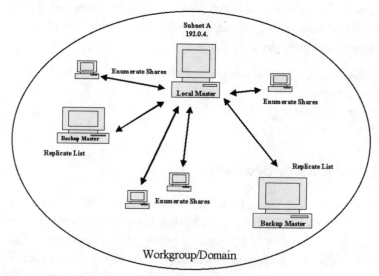

Figure 9.3   *Samba as local master browser*

Domain Master and Cross-Subnet Browsing

Cross-subnet browsing provides a mechanism for unifying share lists in a domain or workgroup that would otherwise have been fragmented due to broadcast barriers between subnets. To enable browsing over subnet boundaries you'll need a system to act as the domain master browser and a WINS server to identify it to the local master servers on each subnet. Remember that WINS uses point-to-point communications not usually blocked by routers.

To make Samba a WINS server, enable the `wins support` parameter and verify that the `wins server` parameter is disabled. *These parameters are mutually exclusive.* Refer to Chapter 8, "Name Service," for additional information related to using Samba in a WINS environment.

```
wins support = yes
```

To point Samba at a remote WINS server, set the value `wins server` parameter to the IP address or DNS name of the WINS server:

```
wins server = <IP address or DNS name>
```

Next you will need a system operating as the domain master browser to collect and synchronize the browse lists from the various local master browsers (Figure 9.4). The domain master can be either a Samba server or an NT domain PDC, but not both. Remember that an NT domain PDC is automatically designated as the domain master browser.

To make Samba the domain master, enable the `domain master`, `local master`, and `preferred master` parameters. Set the `os level` parameter to '65' to exceed the value of all other systems in the workgroup.

```
domain master = yes
local master = yes
preferred master = yes
os level = 65
```

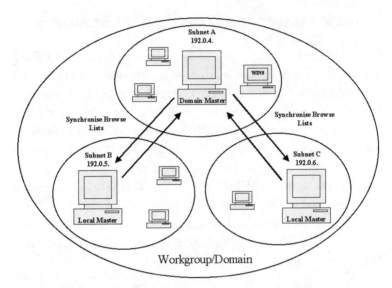

Figure 9.4   *Domain master browser, multi-subnet configuration*

If you already have a Windows NT PDC serving the domain make certain that Samba's domain master parameter is disabled:

```
domain master = no
   local master = yes
   preferred master = yes
   os level = 65
```

Hybrid Cross-Subnet Browsing

In some instances you may need to force announcements or browse list synchronization between subnets for topologies that don't quite fall into the configurations we've examined thus far. There are any number of reasons for doing this, but note that the capability is not available in a native Windows environment.

You can force Samba server announcements to traverse subnet boundaries by using the `remote announce` parameter. The value of the parameter is a list of remote subnet local master browser IP addresses that are the targets for announcements. An arbitrary workgroup name can be matched with each IP address to indicate the workgroup name Samba will use for each subnet (Figure 9.5). If the workgroup name is omitted, the value of the global `workgroup` parameter will be used:

```
remote announce = <IP address list or IP/WORKGROUP list>
```

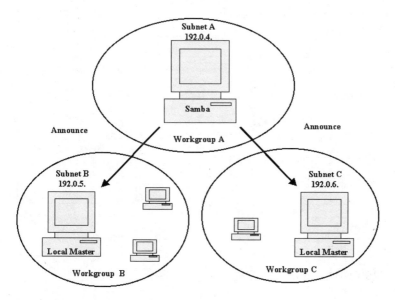

Figure 9.5   *Remote announce configuration*

You can also force browse list synchronization of designated remote subnet local master browsers with Samba using the `remote browse sync` parameter (Figure 9.6). Note that the set of local master browser services must all be running under Samba `nmbd`. This feature is not supported under Windows implementations.

```
remote browse sync = <remote LMB IP address>
```

LAN Manager Browsing

If you need to support browsing for LAN Manager clients like OS/2, add the `lm announce` and `lm interval` parameters to `smb.conf`. A value of *"auto"* for `lm announce` will indicate that `nmbd` should listen for LAN Manager announcements and only respond when required.

```
lm announce = <true, false, auto>
lm interval = <seconds>
```

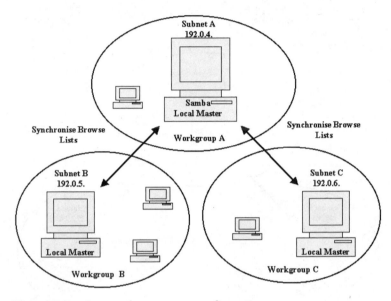

Figure 9.6   *Remote-browse sync configuration*

Problems

Like most distributed network servers, there are a number of things
that can cause problems when incorporating Samba in a browsing
environment. If things aren't working the way you expected, first
check that the various smb.conf parameters are configured correctly. Next verify that you mapped the guest account parameter to a
valid UNIX account for $IPC support. Check the nmbd.log for
anomalies and error messages. Also verify that the argument list used
with nmbd isn't too long and being truncated. Remove spaces
between the argument and value to shorten the command length.

Look at your network configuration. Make sure that you aren't
blocking traffic at routers or network access points. If you have any
Windows for Workgroups clients, don't use network broadcast
addresses that include 0s. Also make sure that you don't have more
than one protocol configured for any Windows master browser
servers. Elections will occur over both protocols. If a server has both

TCP and IPX protocols configured, and the server wins a local master browser election over its IPX channel, TCP browser communications with Samba will be effectively disabled.

For more information regarding Samba browser configuration take a look at the BROWSING.txt and BROWSING-Config.txt distribution documents located in the **samba-<version>/docs/ textdocs** directory.

Summary

- Workgroup and domain clients view available shares via *browser client* tools that request *browse lists* from *master browser* servers.
- Master browsers for each subnet are elected based on *OS level* and *desire* from the set of machines capable of maintaining and serving browse lists. The election losers become *backup browsers* for availability purposes.
- Basic configuration required for Samba participation in a browser environment include designating the netbios name, workgroup name, announce as Windows operating system type, and the announce version. The guest account parameter must also map to a valid UNIX account for $IPC service.

```
workgroup = <workgroup name>
netbios name = <NetBIOS name>
announce as = <NT, Win95, WfW>
announce version = <version number>
guest account = <UNIX account name>
```

- Samba's browser client or server roles are determined by the domain master and local master parameters.

```
domain master = <yes, no>
local master = <yes, no>
```

- Samba can influence the outcome of an election using the os level and preferred master parameters.

```
preferred master = yes
os level = 65
```

- Cross-subnet browsing is enabled by designating a domain master browser to collate browse lists from remote subnet local master browsers. The domain master is identified via WINS service.

```
Wins support = yes
```

or

```
wins server = <IP address or DNS name>
```

- Cross-subnet announcement and list synchronization can also be forced using the non-standard remote announce and remote browse sync parameters.

```
remote announce = <IP address list or IP/WORKGROUP
                    list>
remote browse sync = <remote LMB IP address>
```

- Browse list support for LAN Manager clients like OS/2 is provided by the lm announce and lm interval parameters.

```
lm announce = <true, false, auto>
lm interval = <seconds>
```

Domains

Thus far, we've generalized our Samba configuration discussions so that they would apply equally well in either a workgroup or a domain network model. Samba services like WINS and master browser work equally well for workgroups and domains. In this chapter we'll depart from the generalized track and focus specifically on integrating Samba in a Windows domain.

Domains vs. Workgroups

Windows domains are similar to workgroups in that they represent a group of users, services and computers that collectively share a common namespace. Domains differ from workgroups, in that a domain enforces a common security policy and management structure across its membership. Account directory information is stored in a secure central repository called the *Security Accounts Manager (SAM)*. The SAM database is maintained on the primary domain controller and replicated on each of the backup domain controllers (see Chapter 3). What this means for the system administrator is that there is a central location for managing the accounts, passwords, access controls and policies for the entire domain. End-users benefit from the domain model in by gaining access to all domain resources via a single logon.

Domains improve access security over workgroups because client authentication is performed only once using a secure communication channel with the PDC during domain logon. Once authenticated, client access to resources is governed by applying access controls based on the client's group memberships. Domain groups are a means of categorizing users with similar needs and work profiles.

In contrast, each workgroup client maintains a persistent local cache of accounts and passwords required to access network resource. A separate credential cache is created for each active user and stored in the \windows directory as <username>.PWL. Windows opens the cache file using the associated user's logon password as a key. During connection to a network resource, each entry in the user's credential cache is tried until authentication is either accepted or denied. Credentials stored in these cache files are extremely vulnerable to security threats due to the weak encryption employed and their persistent nature across logons by different workstation users.

Domains also offer a means for authorizing access to resources residing in separate domains through *trusts*. A trust relationship is a link that logically combines two domains into an administrative unit. The trust relationship may be applied one way (*domain A trusts domain B, but domain B does not trust domain A*) or two ways (*domain A and domain B trust each other*).

Samba and Domains

Unlike its extensive WINS and browser implementations, Samba's domain functionality is not quite as feature-inclusive. This is not to say that Samba can't play a part as a client or controller in a domain environment.

A Samba server can participate fully as a client in an NT domain. Samba can also operate as a domain controller within limits. Acting as a domain controller in a Windows 9x environment Samba can support domain logons, logon scripts, user profiles, and system policies. Samba doesn't support SAM database replication nor does it "officially" support remote management via Windows NT domain administration tools. Work is under way to provide Samba PDC functionality in a Windows NT client environment. This effort includes support for interoperation with selected Windows NT domain tools. You will find more about Samba PDC development and the availability of experimental source code later in the chapter.

Domain Client

To add a Samba server as a domain member we must create a machine account and password for the server and register it with the domain's PDC. Begin by stopping the smbd and nmbd daemons on the Samba server. Next, update the server's smb.conf file to reflect the attributes of the target domain (Table 10.1). The security parameter should be set to a value of domain. The netbios name and workgroup parameters must identify the server's NetBIOS name and the domain name respectively. The password server parameter should list the name of the PDC as well as any BDC's for the domain. Because domain logon will require the use of an encrypted password, enable the encrypt passwords parameter. Set the machine password timeout interval to indicate how often smbd should change the machine password. The default value is once a week.

Table 10.1   *Samba Domain Member Parameters*

```
security = domain
netbios name = <NetBIOS name>
workgroup = <domain name>
password server = <PDC BDC1 ... BDCn>
encrypt passwords = true
machine password timeout = <seconds>
```

Don't restart Samba yet. Register the Samba server's NetBIOS name as a domain member using **Server Manager** on the PDC (Figure 10.1). After adding the server name and verifying domain membership, set the machine account password on the Samba server using the smbpasswd command (Example 10.1). The new password will be stored in the /usr/local/samba/private directory as a file named <Domain Name>.<Samba Name>.mac. The mac file name extension stands for *machine account*.

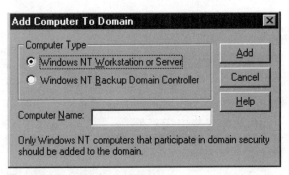

Figure 10.1   *Server Manager*

Example 10.1   *Creating a Domain Server Password*

```
$ smbpasswd -j <Domain Name> -r <PDC Name>.
```

Now it's time to start the smbd and nmbd daemons on the server. Samba should log-on to the domain during initialization. You can verify active membership using Server Manager (Figure 10.2).

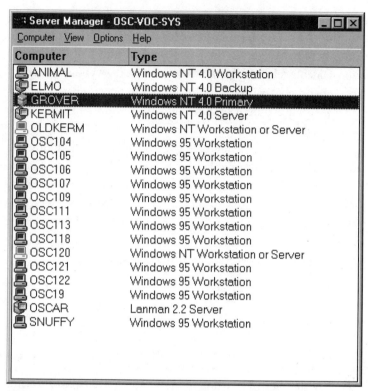

Figure 10.2   *Samba domain membership verification*

When Samba logs on to a domain, it receives the same authentication and authorization information that would be sent to a Windows client. The data includes structures like *Security Identifiers* *(SIDs)* and domain group membership. In future releases of Samba this information will be used for automatic generatation of UNIX UIDs and GIDs. Stay tuned.

Domain Control

Although Samba's domain controller functionality is not quite on a par with Windows NT *yet*, you may still want to consider running Samba as a domain controller for your Windows 9x clients. One reason is that by using Samba as the domain's authentication service, you can collocate UNIX and NetBIOS namespace administration on the same server platform. It may also be that your in-house system administration skills and platform support infrastructure favor running a domain controller under UNIX rather than Windows NT. Whatever the reason, you'll find that Samba will perform adequately as a domain controller in the Windows 9x context. Domain control for Windows NT clients entails additional undocumented protocol support and still lies in the realm of the experimental Samba PDC effort.

To enlist Samba as the domain controller for your Windows 9x domain you'll need to verify that WINS service has been configured and is available (see Chapter 8). You can run WINS under Samba by enabling the `wins support` parameter. If WINS services are provided by another machine, identify the remote server's IP address or DNS name using the `wins server` parameter. Remember that `wins support` and `wins server` are mutually exclusive.

```
wins support = yes
```

or

```
wins server = <IP address or DNS name>
```

Identify the NetBIOS name of the server and the domain name using the `netbios name` and `workgroup` parameters respectively.

```
netbios name = <NetBIOS name>
workgroup = <domain name>
```

You will also need to configure the server to act as the domain master browser (see Chapter 9). Remember that in a Windows NT domain controller world, the PDC is also the domain master browser. Enable the server's `domain master`, `local master`, and `preferred master` parameters and set the `os level` parameter to "65" indicating that Samba is emulating Windows NT Server.

```
os level = 65
domain master = yes
local master = yes
preferred master = yes
```

Next you need to create a `netlogon` a share to support domain logons. This share will be used to store logon scripts and the system policy file, CONFIG.POL (see the "Policies" section later in this chapter). The following is an example netlogin share definition. Make certain that the netlogin share is "read-only" to ensure that the domain's system policies and logon scripts can't be modified by clients:

```
[netlogon]
comment = Network Logon Service
path = /usr/local/samba/lib/netlogon
public = no
writable = no
locking = no
```

Verify the netlogin share configuration by invoking the smbclient command with the -U<username> option. You can include the associated password on the command line by using the "%" character as a delimiter between the username and password:

```
$ smbclient -U <username>[%<password>]
```

If Samba will also be providing a private file store for each client, verify that a homes share is defined in smb.conf (see Chapter 11). The homes share is a special service that provides access to a user's UNIX $HOME directory by referencing the user name when accessing the share. You can also designate that the home directory be mounted as a specified drive letter at login time by setting the logon drive and logon home parameters:

```
[homes]
comment = Home Directories
browseable = no
writable = yes
logon drive = <drive letter>
logon home = \\%N\%U
```

Now you're ready to permit domain logins by enabling the domain logons parameter. You'll also need to verify that the security parameter has a value of *user* and that encrypt passwords is enabled.

```
security = user
encrypt passwords = yes
domain logons = yes
```

Logon Scripts

In Chapter 6 we looked at how the `preexec` and `postexec` parameters can be used to automate execution of commands or scripts when clients connect and disconnect from a share. It is also possible to run a script during domain logon processing using the `logon script` parameter. Using substitution variables in the value of logon script name, it's possible to invoke different logon scripts depending on connecting client SMB information. For example, by using the `%U` parameter as part of the logon script name you can identify per user logon scripts. Make sure you use `crlf` format in your scripts so as not to confuse DOS clients. A sample logon script is listed in Example 10.2. The sample script synchronizes the client's system time with a time server and mounts a shared directory as drive letter `S:`. Combine the use of logon scripts with `preexec` and `postexec` to further tailor domain connect/disconnect processing.

```
logon script = \\%N\netlogin\scripts\%U.bat
```

Example 10.2   *Sample Logon Script*

```
# Sample logon script
ECHO Domain Logon Setup
NET TIME \\<server-name> /YES /SET
NET USE S: \\<server-name>\workspace
```

Roaming Profiles

Most of us spend too much time artistically tailoring our Windows desktops. Our chosen display background, text fonts, application shortcuts, icons, and screen saver all reflect a bit of our cyber persona. Everything has to be in its proper place on the screen. After putting in so much effort, we all get a little irked when our carefully crafted desktop world doesn't automatically follow us as we move from one workstation to the next.

There is a solution to this dilemma called a *roaming profile*, a Windows desktop profile that has been stored on a network drive and copied to the local workstation at logon time. The *profile* itself is a collection of Windows environment settings used in concert with installed applications and folders to create the user's working desktop. Profiles are cached copies of the *Windows Registry Key* HKEY_ CURRENT_USER and stored as a file named **user.DAT** under Windows 9x and NTuser.DAT for Windows NT. The HKEY_ CURRENT_USER structure reflects the desktop preferences set by the current logged in user.

The collection of user profiles is commonly stored by user name in a **PROFILES** directory residing under the system root on the domain controller. When a user logs on to the domain, Windows checks the time stamp of the remote profile stored on the domain controller against a local copy stored on the workstation. The most recent copy is then used to setup the user's initial desktop environment. When the user logs out, the profile is copied back onto the domain controller. Assuming no problems have occurred during domain logout, the most recent copy of the profile will reside on the domain controller and will be available when the user logs on from any domain workstation.

Profiles also provide the system administrator a means for configuring common or default desktop rules for users. If the file extension of the profile file is changed from DAT to MAN, the profile becomes a mandatory profile and will be used to set the initial desktop environment. The end-user can modify the desktop during the session, but those changes will not be reflected in the mandatory profile stored on the domain controller.

Roaming profiles are designated in Samba by the logon path parameter. The default path is to store the profile in the user's home directory. Due to the problem that Windows clients may leave the home directory mounted after user logout, it is recommended to specify an alternate repository for storing roaming profiles. A simple solution is to create a separate share for storing roaming profiles (Example 10.3).

```
logon path = <profile path>
```

Example 10.3　*Alternate Roaming Profile Share*

```
logon path = \\%N\profiles\%U
[profiles]
        path = /usr/local/samba/profiles
        create mode = 600
        directory mode = 0770
        browseable = no
        writeable = yes
```

You may also experience problems resolving profile names due to file name case. It is recommended that you also enable the `preserve case` and `short case preserve` parameters and disable the `case sensitive` parameter:

```
preserve case = yes
short case preserve = yes
case sensitive = no
```

System Policies

System policies represent the last stick available to the system administrator for tailoring the working environment of domain users. A system policy is a union of user profile and system profile. The system profile is reflected in the `HKEY_LOCAL_MACHINE` key branch of the registry. The system policy is a means for ensuring consistent environment policy for users, groups and machines. System settings enforced by the system policy include control panel access, desktop schemes, Windows Shell, access to system tools, and application configuration.

The domain administrator sets system policy values using the *System Policy Editor*, `poledit.exe` (Figure 10.3). The new policy is saved as a file named `config.pol` in Windows 9x and `NTconfig.pol` in Windows NT. You can get a copy of `poledit.exe` from the Windows distribution CD.

To use system policies in Samba, you'll need to create a `config.pol` file on a Windows 9x workstation. After setting your environment preferences, save the file and copy it into Samba's `netlogin` share.

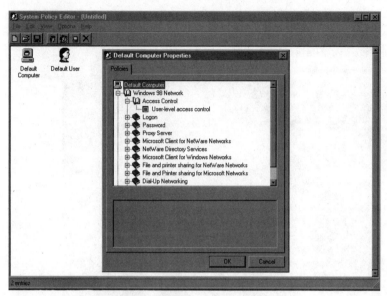

Figure 10.3   *System Policy Editor, poledit.exe*

Windows Client Setup

Now that you've finished configuring Samba to operate as a domain controller, you'll need to configure the domain login settings on each of your Windows 9x workstations. If multiple users will use individual domain workstations, you'll need to enable support for multiple user profiles on these computers. Do this clicking on **Start → Settings → Control Panel → Users** (Figure 10.4) and **Start → Settings → Control Panel → Passwords** (Figure 10.5). After completing profile setup, don't restart your computer until you finished configuring domain logon properties. Identify the user set and whether default or individual user profiles will be supported.

Enable domain logons in Windows 9x by selecting **Start → Settings → Control Panel → Network** from the desktop. Make sure that Client for Microsoft Networks is installed. Open the **properties** tab. Set the "Logon to Windows NT domain" box and enter the name of the domain (Figure 10.6). Apply the changes and restart. The Windows Logon box should now display user, password, and domain options. The first time each user logs on to the domain he/she will be asked about saving the user profile. Each user should select **Yes**. Check the Samba roaming profiles store to verify that a profile was created for the new user.

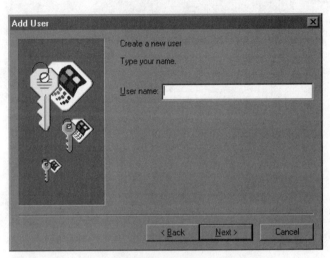

Figure 10.4   *Control Panel → Users*

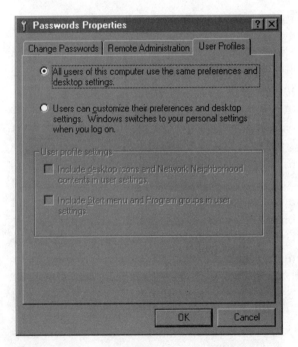

Figure 10.5   *Control Panel → Passwords*

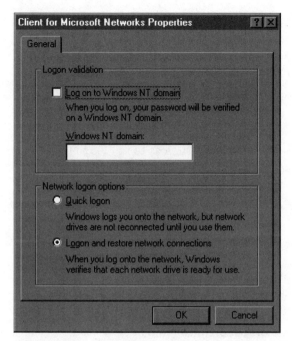

Figure 10.6   *Client for Microsoft Networks Properties*

Primary Domain Controller

In the chapter introduction I mentioned the Samba PDC development project. This idea is to extend Samba's domain controller capability to include Windows NT PDC functionality. A fair amount of work has already been completed. Unsupported versions of the Samba PDC-enabled code are available from the Samba download sites for evaluation and testing. According to the latest Samba *NT Domain FAQ*, here is information on which PDC features are available and which are not.

Currently included features are:

- The ability to act as a PDC for Windows NT 3.51 Service Pack 5 and Windows NT 4.0 Service Pack 4 clients. This includes adding NT machines to the domain and authenticating users logging into the domain.
- Domain account can be viewed using the "User Manager for Domains."

- Viewing resources on the Samba PDC via Server Manager from an NT client
- Windows 95 clients will allow user-level security to be set, but will not currently allow browsing of accounts.
- Machine account password updates
- Changing of user passwords from an NT client
- User name <-> RID mapping
- Some tools work with this such as the NT Sec tools from Pedestal software.
- Some tools, like `explorer.exe`, do not work.
- Partial support for Windows NT group and user name mapping
- Support for a LDAP password database back-end.

Release of a stable, full-featured Samba PDC is currently slated for version 2.1. The NT domain client code is available beginning with version 2.0. The following are not currently available in the NTDOM PDC support but eventually will be:

- Trust relationships.
- PDC <=> BDC integration.
- Network printing (see FAQ question 2.5 for a workaround).
- Windows NT ACLs (on the Samba shares).

Obtaining the Source

The best way to get the latest information about which features have been implemented is to obtain the latest source code from the *HEAD* branch of the CVS code tree. To download a copy of the Samba Domain Controller source code, you'll need a copy of cvs (**http://download.cyclic.com**). Use cvs to log in to the Samba CVS source server and update your copy of the Samba source code.

```
$ cvs -d :pserver:cvs@samba.org:/cvsroot login
 password: cvs
$ cvs -d :pserver:cvs@samba.org:/cvsroot co samba
$ cvs update -d -P
```

Configuration

Build and install the source as you would a standard distribution (see Chapter 5). It's a good idea to install the binaries using an alternate directory tree for testing and evaluation purposes. Configure Samba as outlined in the previous section describing domain control for Windows 9x environments and start the server. The first time the server is invoked it will create a file in the /usr/local/samba/private directory to identify the domain SID. The file name is <*domain name*>.SID.

With the server up and running, set up machine trust accounts for each member of the domain. The machine trust accounts are similar to user accounts with the exception that a "**$**" character is appended to the account name. First add a <*machine client name*>$ entry in the UNIX /etc/passwd file using the following format:

```
<NetBIOS-name>$:*:<uid>:<gid>:<Client Description>: \
/dev/null:/bin/false
```

Once the account has been added to UNIX, add the account to Samba's password file:

```
$ smbpasswd -a -m <NetBIOS-name>$
```

Finally, map Windows accounts and groups to their UNIX counterparts. This is done by specifying the location of mapping files with the domain user map, domain group map, and local group map parameters. Table 10.2 lists each parameter with the associated format for pairing the UNIX and Windows accounts and groups.

Table 10.2 *UNIX/Windows Account and Group Maps*

```
domain user map = <path>
Format:        UNIXuser = [\\domain\]NTuser

domain group map =
Format:        UNIXgroup = NTgroup

local group map =
Format:        UNIXgroup = [BUILTIN\]NTgroup
*BUILTIN indicates default NT groups like "Administrator".
```

Windows 2000

Windows 2000 builds upon the Windows domain model by organizing domains into a hierarchical tree structure supporting both central and distributed administration (Figure 10.7). The collection of domains and administrative policies is managed by Windows 2000 *Active Directory*. Active Directory is a combination of the legacy NT domain security architecture augmented with a set of open technologies that include Lightweight Directory Access Protocol (LDAP), Kerberos Version 5.0, and Internet-style Domain Name Service (DNS). Active Directory supports a mixed environment of Windows 2000 and Windows NT 4.0 domain controllers. Back-level clients can still log on using NT LAN Manager challenge/response authentication.

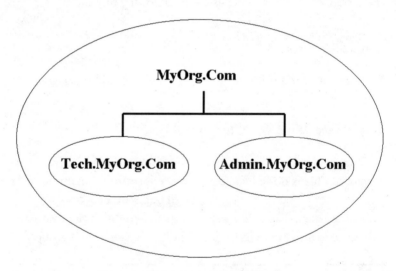

Figure 10.7   *Windows 2000 domain tree structure*

It is still a bit early to tell how Samba can participate in the Windows 2000 domain, tree, and forest model. Keep an eye on the Samba discussion archives concerning the latest Windows 2000 and Samba interoperability issues.

Summary

- Domains are similar to workgroups but provide additional functionality and security via a shared security policy.
- Samba supports full domain client compatibility and domain controller services for Windows 9x environments.
- To configure Samba as a domain client:

  1. Stop `smbd` and `nmbd`.
  2. Update `smb.conf`.

  ```
      security = domain
      netbios name = <NetBIOS name>
      workgroup = <domain name>
      password server = <PDC BDC1 ... BDCn>
      encrypt passwords = true
  machine password timeout = <seconds>
  ```

  3. Register the server using Windows Server Manager.
  4. Set server machine account password:

  ```
  $ smbpasswd -j <Domain Name> -r <PDC Name>
  ```

  5. Restart **smbd** and **nmbd**.

- To configure Samba as a Windows 9x domain controller:

  1. Enable WINS support, identify server name, and workgroup name.

  ```
  wins support = yes
  netbios name = <server name>
  workgroup = <domain name>
  ```

  2. Configure Samba as the domain master browser.

  ```
  os level = 64
    domain master = yes
    local master = yes
  preferred master = yes
  ```

  3. Setup netlogin, homes, and profiles shares.

```
[netlogin]
[homes]
[profilesl]
logon script = \\%N\netlogin\scripts\%U.bat
logon drive = <drive letter>
logon home = \\%N\%U
logon path = <profile path>
```

4. Set domain logon parameters.

```
security = user
encrypt passwords = yes
domain logons = yes
```

5. Create System Policy using poledit.exe on a Windows
   9x machine and copy to Samba netlogin share.
6. Enable user profiles and domain logons on the Windows
   9x clients.

- Samba PDC support is under development. Experimental
  source code is available from the cvs HEAD source tree.

11

Sharing Files

"Rumors of my assimilation have been greatly exaggerated."

Picard

It is Samba's job to act as arbiter when *assimilating* UNIX and Windows resources. Samba's melding of the OS protocol psyches constructs a logical communication channel for sharing files and printers residing in each of the two architectures. Samba resource sharing services augment simple data transfer by incorporating features like name and attribute mapping, locking and caching, and multiple levels of access control. As with all the service definitions we've discussed thus far, Samba share service behavior is directed through parameters specified in the smb.conf configuration file.

File Shares

Probably the most common form of resource sharing under Samba is providing Windows client access to UNIX files and directories. File shares are defined in the services section of smb.conf. With the exception of the special [homes] share, each file share is uniquely identified by a share name enclosed in square brackets, [share name]. The share name is minimally followed by a path parameter defining the shared directory path. It is also a good idea to include a short description of the share specified by the **comment** parameter.

```
[share name]
comment = <text description>
path = <directory path>
```

Additional parameters may be added to each file share section to tailor file name mapping preferences, set read/write permissions, enforce access control and specify special locking options. Parameters like preexec and postexec can be used in a file share definition to induce special pre and post connect processing. For example, you might use root preexec to request a mount for removable media when a share is accessed (Example 11.1). An unmount would follow at disconnect time using the root postexec parameter.

Example 11.1   *Removable Media File Share*

```
[cdrom]
path = /mnt/cdrom
comment = Removable CDROM Share
browseable = yes
read only = yes
root preexec = /usr/sbin/mount -o ro /dev/cd0 /mnt/cdrom
root postexec = /usr/sbin/umount /mnt/cdrom
```

Homes Share

The [homes] section is a special share service provided by Samba to allow Windows client users to access their UNIX home directories. When an SMB connection setup request is received, Samba first scans the set of specifically named shares. If a match is not found, it will then scan the passwd database attempting to locate a match for the client user name. If a user name match is found and the client has supplied the correct password, Samba grants access to a temporary [user name] share created by cloning the [homes] section definitions. If a path parameter has not been supplied, the user's home directory path is used as specified in the UNIX passwd database.

A sample [homes] definition is provided in Example 11.2. Take special note of the write access parameters used in the example [homes] definition. The use of write list = %S versus writeable = yes eliminates the possibility that another user could gain read access to a home directory set with world read permission.

Example 11.2   *Sample [homes] Section Definition*

```
[homes]
comment = User Home Directories
browseable = no
writeable = no
write list = %S
```

[homes] user directory shares can be accessed by providing the user name as the share name or by specifying *homes* as the share name.

In the latter case, the user name is derived from the requesting client setup request. This feature is useful when configuring a logon script to setup a common desktop environment on a multi-user workstation. Be aware that some Windows clients will not unmount the home directory share when a user logs out. You may want to force an unmount as part of the logout environment clean-up process:

```
C:\ NET USE H: \\<server name>\<user name>
```

```
C:\ NET USE H: \\<server name>\homes
```

Other [homes] section considerations include specifying an alternate user directory using the path parameter to separate UNIX user directories and Windows client user directories (Example 11.3). Also, note that even though the browseable parameter is disabled, individual users will still see their home directories listed as folders in a browse list.

Example 11.3   *[homes] Share with Alternate Directory Path*
```
[homes]
comment = User Home Directories
browseable = no
writeable = no
write list = %S
path = /home/samba/%u
```

Sites that use NIS managed directory servers can route [homes] connections to the appropriate remote directory server by enabling the nis homedir parameter and identifying the *NIS map* with the homedir map parameter. The remote directory server must also be running Samba. The home directory will be mounted directly from the directory server:

```
nis homedir = <true, false>
homedir map = <NIS map name>
```

Access Control

In Chapter 6, we looked at some of the access controls that can be applied to Samba shares. We'll review them here, focusing on how they affect access to file shares specifically. Table 11.1 lists the set of access control parameters we'll cover in the next few sections of the text.

Table 11.1 *Useful Access Control Parameters*

By Host

hosts allow	Allow/restrict hosts
hosts deny	

By User and Group

username	Restrict/allow users
valid users	
invalid users	
only user	
force user	
guest ok	Public access
guest only	
guest account	
group	Enforce named group rights
force group	

By File Operation

read only	Read-only access
read list	
writeable	Write access
write list	
force security mode	Specify permissions
force create mode	
force directory mode	
force directory security mode	
security mask	
create mask	
directory mask	
directory security mask	

continued on next page

Table 11.1	*Useful Access Control Parameters*
Hide	
`veto files`	Hide/restrict specified files
`hide files`	
`hide dot files`	
`delete veto files`	
`dont descend`	

Browse Rights

The least-effective method of access control is security by obscurity.
I mention this because many sites will use the `browseable` parameter to hide a share and assume that is sufficient to protect it from
unauthorized access. They subscribe to a cyber philosophical twist
on old sayings like, *"What your users don't know can't hurt you"* and
"User ignorance is system administrator bliss". There are certainly good
reasons for making a share nonbrowseable. Just remember that
although a share doesn't show up in a browse list, users can still
access it if they know the name a priori:

```
browseable = <yes, no>
```

Host Access

The most basic form of Samba access control is by host name or IP
address. Use the `hosts allow` and `hosts deny` parameters in the
global and share sections of `smb.conf` to restrict access to those
hosts that are trusted members of your workgroup or domain. You
can specify computers by name, IP number, or IP group by using an
IP class value or subnet mask. The `except` keyword can be used in
conjunction with group values like a subnet mask to exclude individual or groups of machines (Example 11.4).

Example 11.4   *Restricting Access by Host*

```
hosts allow = 192.168. except 192.168.0.10

hosts deny = frodo, bilbo

hosts allow = 149.125.10.0/255.255.255.0
```

User and Group Access

A finer level of access restraint can be applied at the user level. Samba allows you to limit right of entry to specific individuals through the username, only user, valid users, and invalid users parameters (Example 11.5). Per the particular parameter employed, the client-supplied user name is checked against the associated user list before access is granted or denied. If the user name is prefixed with an "@" sign, or an "&" sign it is assumed to correspond to an NIS netgroup. If it is prefixed with a "+" sign, the name is checked against the UNIX group file.

Example 11.5   *Restricting Access by User Name*

```
invalid users = root system +wheel

only user = fred
```

The following rules are applied when a client requests access to a share or service. Access is granted if:

- An unrestricted client passes a user name and password that maps to a permitted UNIX account name.
- A client previously registered a user name with the server and follows up by supplying a valid password.
- The client's NetBIOS name and previously used user name are checked against the supplied password.
- A client with a previously validated user name/password pair supplies a validation token to the server.

- The share is configured with the user list parameter and the client supplies a valid password for one of the usernames in the list.
- A share is configured with a guest account parameter and the client supplies a valid guest account name.

Sometimes you will want to make a share available to anyone. Adding the guest ok or guest only parameters to a share section definition will accomplish this. Note that even though you are granting public access to the resource, you will still want to restrict operation privileges on the share by mapping guest access to a valid UNIX account. Indicate the desired user account name as a value to the guest account parameter. A good candidate account with limited privileges is the nobody account which is commonly used for UNIX anonymous access services (Example 11.6).

Example 11.6   *Restricting Guest Access*

```
guest ok = true

guest account = nobody
```

Privileges and Permissions

Now that we've narrowed connection rights down to an explicit community of client users and machines, we'll want to bind the set of operations permitted on file and directory objects contained within the share. This is accomplished by indicating whether a user has read or write privileges based on effective UNIX user and group identifiers, and how UNIX owner, group and world permissions are specified for manipulating files and directories. Keep in mind that Samba must honor UNIX permissions regardless of the parameter specifications designated for the share in smb.conf.

Read/write permissions can be specified at the share level or user level using the readonly, read list, writeable, and write list parameters. If the user name is prefixed with an "@" sign or a "&" sign it is assumed to correspond to an NIS netgroup. If it is prefixed with a "+" sign, the name is checked against the UNIX group file. The "+" and "@"/"&" characters can be combined to indicate that a check be made against both UNIX groups file and NIS netgroups.

```
writeable = <yes, no>
```

```
write list = <comma separated user list>
```

```
readonly = <yes, no>
```

```
read list = <comma separated user list>
```

Due to the wide range of access control attributes employed by DOS, LAN Manger, Windows 9x and Windows NT clients, Samba requires a set of mechanisms to ensure that these attributes are reflected in corresponding UNIX file and directory permissions. This is carefully achieved through a set of *mask* or *mode* (synonym for mask) parameters that guarantee appropriate application of UNIX permissions.

There are two levels of masking that can be applied when a client creates a file or directory within a Samba file share. The first set of mask parameters are *bit-wise AND'ed* with the UNIX permission bits resulting from the mapping of DOS modes or NT access control attributes. Any bit not matching the mask will be removed from the resulting UNIX permission bits when the file or directory is created. The first-level mask parameters include `create mask` (DOS), `directory mask` (DOS), `security mask` (NT), and `directory security mask` (NT). Values for each of these parameters are designated as an octal mask:

```
create mask = <default=0744>
```

```
directory mask = <default=0755>
```

```
security mask = <default=create mask>
```

```
    directory security mask = <default=directory mask>
```

The next level of file and directory permission parameters allows you to *force* the setting of permission bits through *bit-wise OR'ing* with the results of the first level parameters. This ensures that certain owner, group and world permission bits will always be applied when a file or directory is created. Second-level parameters include `force create mode` (DOS), `force directory mode` (DOS), `force security mode` (NT), and `force directory security mode` (NT). Refer to the `smb.conf` (5) man page for additional information.

```
force create mode = <default=000>

force directory mode = <default=000>

force security mode = <default=force create mode>

force directory security mode = <default=force directory mode>
```

In some instances you may want to force the assignment of a particular effective UNIX user or group to be used when operating on objects in the share. This is useful when multiple users are sharing access to a file share. By specifying a UNIX *user name* and *group name* as values to the `force user` and `force group` parameters, you can ensure that all file operations on the service will be performed using the named user and group for permissions checking and assignment:

```
force user = <user name>

force group = <group name>
```

As of Samba 2.0.5, the `force group` parameter allows a "+" character to be added as a prefix to the group name value. What this means is that a connecting user only operates under the specified effective group if it is already listed as a member of that group in the `/etc/groups` file (Example 11.7). All other users will operate under their own default primary UNIX groups.

Example 11.7   *2.0.5 Force Group Enhancement*

```
force group = +sys
```

Power users that require full administrative privileges for a share are designated with the `admin users` parameter. This basically gives these users *root* privileges when operating on files and directories within the share.

```
admin users = <user list>
```

Hiding Files & Directories

Another form of security by obscurity is facilitated through Samba's ability to hide files and directories from SMB clients. For practical purposes it may be prudent to hide things like UNIX dot files in [homes] shares. UNIX dot files can be hidden by enabling the hide dot files parameter. Other UNIX files and directories can be hidden using the hide files and dont decend parameters. The hide files parameter accepts a list of "/" separated file names or file patterns. File patterns use the "?" and "*" characters to wild-card single characters or filename/extension similar to the way they are used in DOS (Example 11.8). The dont decend parameter accepts a list of comma-separated directory names that are off-limits to connected clients. The dont decend parameter is also useful in eliminating recursive directory lookup loops caused by symbolic links:

```
hide dot files = <yes, no>

hide files = <file pattern / file pattern / ...>

dont decend = <directory list>
```

Example 11.8   *Hide Files by Pattern*

```
hide files = *.mbx / pine.*
```

Hiding files and directories does not restrict access if the client user already knows the hidden file or path name. To restrict access to hidden files and directories use the veto files parameter. Like the hide files parameter, veto files accepts a list of "/" separated file/directory names or file/directory patterns with support for "?" and "*" wild card characters. To allow clients the ability to delete a directory that contains files restricted by a `veto files` parameter, enable the `delete veto files` parameter:

```
veto files = <file pattern / file pattern>

delete veto files = <yes, no>
```

DOS and Windows File Attributes

UNIX *owner*, *group*, and *world* execute permission bits don't have a counterpart in the DOS and Windows world. This is because execute permission is implied by a file name extension of EXE. Likewise, UNIX file attributes don't include anything like the *archive*, *system*, and *hidden* attributes used by DOS and Windows. Samba's solution to this dilemma is to allow mapping of the DOS/Windows *archive*, *system*, and *hidden* attributes to the UNIX *owner*, *group*, and *world* execute bits. Attribute mapping is switched on or off by the `map archive`, `map system`, and `map hidden` parameters.

`map archive = <yes, no>`   UNIX owner execute bit

`map system = <yes, no>`   UNIX group execute bit

`map hidden = <yes, no>`   UNIX world execute bit

Windows NT Access Control Lists (ACLs) are mapped into UNIX permission bits by enabling the `nt acl support` parameter.

`nt acl support = <yes, no>`

File Name Mangling

Along with the mapping of access control attributes and permissions, Samba also translates file and path names into their respective UNIX, DOS, and Windows forms (Table 11.2). In general, the translation entails applying an algorithm (Table 11.4) to convert long case-sensitive UNIX file names into case-insensitive DOS 8.3 format. The method is similar to, but different from, that employed by

Windows 9x and Windows NT when transforming long file names (LFN) into a DOS 8.3 representation. The ability of a client to support LFN or DOS 8.3 format is negotiated during session setup.

Samba also maintains a cache of recently used mangled file names. This is done to prevent problems related to reverse name mangling. Many DOS or Windows applications may attempt to create a UNIX file using a mangled name form during a rename operation. For example, text editors that open a file, rename the previous version using a BAK extension, and then rewrite the modified file with the original extension. You can specify the number of cached names using the mangled stack parameter.

```
mangled stack = <integer>
```

Table 11.2   *File Name Characteristics*

UNIX

File name 255 chars

All chars except "/" and ESC

Mixed case, case sensitive

DOS (pre 7.0), Windows for Workgroups

File name 8.3 chars

All chars except \ / : * ? " < > |

Upper case translation, case insensitive

Windows 9x, Windows NT

File name 127 chars

All chars except \ / : * ? " < > |

Win32, LFN, Universal Naming Convention (UNC) names

Win 2K filenames

File name 255 chars

All chars except \ / : * ? " < > |

Win32, LFN, Universal Naming Convention (UNC) names

You can easily tailor different name mangling translations for each share using the parameters listed in Table 11.3. Example 11.9

demonstrates a UNIX-to-DOS 8.3 transformation with UNIX and Windows views of the same UNIX home directory.

Table 11.3   *Samba Name Mangling Parameters*

mangled names	Enable/Disable name mangling of non-DOS format UNIX names into DOS 8.3 form.
mangle case	Enable/Disable case mangling of characters not of the default case.
mangling char	Designate an alternative mangle character.
mangled map	Specify individual file name translations. Each translation pair is enclosed in parentheses. Example. (*.HTML *HTM). Multiple translation sets can be defined by separating each parentheses-enclosed pair by a blank.
case sensitive	Designates whether file names are case sensitive.
default case	Set default file case to upper or lower.
preserve case	New files are created using case passed by client or default case.
short preserve case	New DOS 8.3 format files are created using case passed by client or default case.
strip dot	Remove trailing period from UNIX file names with no extension.

Table 11.4   *Samba File Name Mangling Rules*

1. The first five alphanumeric characters of the UNIX file name are uppercased and used as the root of the new file name. Non-alphanumeric characters are ignored.

2. A "~" or the character designated by mangling char parameter is appended to the new five-character root file name and is followed with a two-character hash of the original file name without any extension.

3. The first three characters of the original file extension are uppercased and used as the new file extension. If there are no periods in the original file name, then no extension is applied.

4. If not specified as hidden, file names with a leading period (UNIX hidden files) are treated as above but have the leading period removed and have an extension of three "_" characters.

Example 11.9   *Mangled UNIX Directory Listing*

UNIX

```
(deroest) ls -l

-rw-------  1 deroest  user     1379 Jan 29  1998 .kshrc
-rwxr-x---  1 deroest  daemon    669 Sep 17  1997 .login
-rwx------  1 deroest  daemon     68 Aug 14  1989 .logout
-rwxr-x---  1 deroest  daemon    615 Sep 17  1997 .profile
drwxr-xr-x  2 deroest  daemon    512 Oct 20 20:43 .ssh
drwx------  2 deroest  user      512 Mar 24  1997 News
drwxr-xr-x  5 deroest  daemon    512 Oct 30  1997 bin
-rw-------  1 deroest  daemon   2210 Apr 30 13:59 dead.letter
drwx------  2 deroest  user      512 Mar 24  1997 etc
drwxr-xr-x  4 deroest  staff     512 Mar 24  1997 info
drwx------  2 deroest  daemon    512 Mar 24  1997 mail
-rwxr-xr-x  1 deroest  daemon    716 Oct 21 15:34 mbuf.sh
drwxr-xr-x  2 deroest  daemon    512 Jul 21 14:52 src
drwxr-x---  2 deroest  user    27648 Oct 15 14:35 tmp
```

DOS

```
D:\>dir

Volume in drive D is DEROEST
Directory of D:\

KSHRC~TG ___    1,379  01-29-98  3:12p .kshrc
LOGIN~SY ___     669   09-17-97  8:09a .login
LOGOU~KI ___     68    08-14-89  9:42p .logout
PROFI~GU ___     615   09-17-97  8:09a .profile
SSH~OO   ___    <DIR>  10-20-99  8:43p .ssh
tmp      <DIR>  10-15-99  2:35p tmp
info     <DIR>  03-24-97  2:47a info
etc      <DIR>  03-24-97  2:47a etc
```

continued on next page

Example 11.9   *Mangled UNIX Directory Listing*

```
News     <DIR>   03-24-97   2:47a News
mail     <DIR>   03-24-97   2:47a mail
src      <DIR>   07-21-99   2:52p src
bin      <DIR>   10-30-97  12:07p bin
mbuf     sh       716  10-21-99   3:34p mbuf.sh
DEAD~ZC  LET    2,210  04-30-99   1:59p dead.letter
```

CRLF/LF Conversion

Another problem when translating file attributes between UNIX and DOS/Windows involves CRLF/LF conversion. Unfortunately there is no reliable way to determine which files need conversion and which do not. You cannot rely on file name extensions like TXT or DOC. Samba operates on the premise that files are not to be modified automatically to ensure that files are not mistakenly damaged by erroneous conversions. Note that some operating systems like Linux may automatically convert CD-ROM files based on file type. Use the `conv=binary` mount option to disable conversions for CDROM shares managed by Samba.

Jim Barry has written an excellent drag-and-drop CRLF/LF converter for Windows called `fixcrlf` that can be used to convert files as needed. To covert a file just drag the file from Windows Explorer onto the `fixcrlf` icon. You can download a copy of `fixcrlf` from one of the Samba archive sites: **ftp://samba.org/pub/samba/ contributed/fixcrlf.zip**

Locking

Sharing files in a distributed environment always involves locking mechanisms for serialization and notification of updates. Samba supports two basic types, DOS/Windows *share mode* locking and *opportunistic locks (oplocks)*.

Share mode locking is enabled by the `share modes` parameter. Share mode locking is implemented using either shared memory (fast) or file locks (slow) because there is no general UNIX counterpart for share mode operations. Samba implements `DENY_DOS`, `DENY_ALL`, `DENY_READ`, `DENY_WRITE`, `DENY_NONE`, and `DENY_FCB` lock requests (Table 11.5).

```
share modes = <yes, no>
```

Table 11.5   *Samba Share Modes*

`DENY_DOS`	DOS compatibility mode. Additional opens by the same client are allowed.
`DENY_FCB`	File compatibility mode. `DENY_DOS` open then set open to read/write. If first open client is writing then no other client reads are allowed. If first client is read-only, then additional client reads are allowed.
`DENY_ALL`	All other open requests are denied.
`DENY_READ`	Write-only opens are allowed.
`DENY_WRITE`	Read- only opens are allowed.
`DENY_NONE`	Additional open requests are allowed.

Opportunistic locking is a locking method that allows Windows clients aggressively to cache file data blocks on the local client. Three types of oplocks might be requested by a LAN Manager or Windows client. The first is called an *exclusive oplock*. This permits a client to obtain exclusive access to a file. The second type is a *batch oplock*. A file locked with a batch oplock allows the client to keep a file open on the server even though a local application on the client may have closed the file. The third type of oplock is a *level II oplock* and permits multiple client read access to a file with no writers. Enabling Samba oplock support (default) can realize file IO performance improvements of up to 30 percent. See the `smb.conf` (5) man page for details on lock parameters.

```
oplocks=<yes, no>
```

Samba release 2.0.5 introduced support for level II oplocks. The `level2 oplocks` allow a read/write client to downgrade its oplock to `readonly` when additional clients request access to a file.

```
level2 oplocks = <yes, no>
```

For specific instances when you want to allow multiple clients to request oplocks on the same file, you can direct Samba to permit multiple oplock request by enabling the `fake oplocks` parameter. *Keep in mind that if this option is permitted on **writeable** shares, you may end up with data corruption.* Permitting multiple oplock requests on `readonly` shares can result in significant performance improvement due to local client file caching.

```
fake oplocks = <yes, no>
```

Problems can occur if the data are accessed via non-Samba controlled interfaces. The Samba client holding the oplock isn't aware of access by the non-Samba application. Support for oplocks can be turned off for specific files by specifying one or more file-matching patterns as values to the `veto oplocks files` parameter.

```
veto oplocks files = /*.mbx/
```

You can also turn off oplock support in Windows 9x and Windows NT by modifying the system registry. This isn't a recommended procedure, because disabling all oplock support may adversely affect some Windows applications. If you choose to disable oplocks on the client side, refer to the Samba distribution document `File-Caching.txt`. A registry update file is also available in the Samba distribution for Windows 9x and Windows NT, `Win9x-CacheHandling.reg`, and `NT4-Locking.reg`.

Another method of dealing with the unknown client access problem is facilitated by kernel-level oplocks supported under some UNIX implementations. When another process, like NFS, touches a file that has been oplocked by Samba, the lock is broken or downgraded per the specified oplock options.

```
kernel oplocks = <yes, no>
```

Byte-range locking within a file can be enabled/disabled with the `ole locking compatibility` parameter. Samba implements byte-range locking by invoking the `fcntl()` system call. `fcntl()` tracks location range using a 32 bit signed integer. Windows OLE2 clients use the 32nd bit of the range value as a semphore that may cause range value problems for some UNIX and NFS systems.

```
ole locking compatibility = <yes, no>
```

Symbolic Links

DOS and Windows clients don't support cross-file linking similar to UNIX symbolic links. Samba allows clients to follow UNIX symbolic links by enabling the follow links parameter. Symbolic link targets that reside outside a share's directory tree can be accessed from a client by enabling the wide links parameter.

```
follow symlinks  = <yes, no>

wide links = <yes, no>
```

Limiting Load

At times when a share becomes too popular for existing server resources, you can limit the number of concurrent connections with the max connections parameter. This feature might also be useful for checking concurrent accesses due to licensing restrictions:

```
max connections = <integer>
```

Summary

- Minimum definition of a file share will include the share name enclosed in square brackets and a directory path parameter. A comment parameter describing the share is also desirable.

  ```
  [share name]
  comment = <text description>
  path = <directory path>
  ```

- Special [homes] file share section allows users to access their UNIX $HOME directory from and SMB client.
- Access control parameters can be applied to a file share restricting access by host, user, and privilege.

- Non-browseable and hidden file parameters remove visibility of a share or file but do not restrict access if the share or file name is known by the client.

- File access mode and mask parameters must honor the underlying UNIX permissions.

- DOS/Windows *archive*, *system*, and *hidden* attributes can be mapped into UNIX *owner*, *group*, and *world* execute bits with the map archive, map system, and map hidden parameters.

- Samba file name mangling is used to convert case sensitive UNIX long file names into DOS 8.3 format. Conversion mapping can be tailored per file share.

- Automatic CRLF/LF file text conversion is not supported because Samba cannot accurately determine when a file should be converted. A CRLF/LF tool is available for allowing clients to convert files as needed: **ftp://samba.org/pub/ samba/contributed/fixcrlf.zip**

- Samba supports two basic locking mechanisms. DOS *share mode* locking and *windows opportunistic locking (oplocks)*.

- Samba provides access to UNIX symbolic linked files by enabling the follow symlinks parameter. Link targets that reside outside a share's scope can be made accessible using the wide links parameter.

12

Print Shares

Samba is a veritable Swiss army knife when it comes
to printing subsystem interfaces. Printing is one
area where there are substantial differences between
the various UNIX implementations: daemons, configuration files, and commands. Samba does an out-
standing job of supporting most of the popular
UNIX printing subsystems. Once Samba knows the
operating system type, enabling Windows and LAN
Manager printing to local UNIX printers is a breeze
(or at least a small gale).

Global Print Parameters

First and foremost when you are configuring Samba as a print server, identify the operating system type. This enlightens Samba about
the nature of the commands and configuration files that will be used
in interoperation with the print spooling system. The operating system type is identified by the global `printing` parameter. Supported
operating systems include AIX, BSD, HPUX, LPRNG, PLP,
QNX, SOFTQ, and SYSV.

```
printing = <os type>
```

Once the operating system type is known, Samba needs to know
the location of the printer configuration file. The path name of the
printer configuration file is specified by the global `printcap name`
parameter. Samba matches client printer access requests against the
queue names listed in the configuration file. Valid targets for a match
include all printer aliases defined in the printer database. Default values for `printcap name`, based on the specified operating system
type, include `/etc/printcap` for BSD systems, `/etc/qconfig` for
AIX, and `lpstat` for SYSV systems. In the case of SYSV systems,
Samba invokes the `lpstat` command to obtain the list of available
printers:

```
printcap name = <printer config file>
```

If you don't want to make all the printers listed in your printer
configuration file available for client access, consider using an alternate configuration file for your workgroup or domain. Make a copy
of the default printer configuration file using a different file name or
path. Remove those printer definitions to which you wish to restrict
access. Use the copy configuration file as the value of the printcap
name parameter. Don't forget that you'll need to keep synchronized
the printer configurations that reside in each file.

To make the set of available printers visible to browsing, enable
the global load printers parameter. The default setting, yes, will add
all printers listed in the printer configuration file to the browse list.

```
load printers = <yes, no>
```

Print Share

Print shares are defined either with an explicit share name enclosed in square brackets or by using the special [printers] share (next section). A minimal print share definition will include a path parameter designating the location of a world writeable spooling directory. It must also be set printable or the server will not load the configuration. Set the writeable parameter to no in order to restrict non-spooling related writes to the share. If you want to allow public access to the printer, enable the guest ok parameter and verify that guest account is set to a known UNIX account. If the chosen share name does not match an entry in the UNIX printer configuration file, use the printer parameter to designate a valid printer name.

```
[print share name]
comment = <text description>
printer = <printcap printer name>
path = <spooling directory>
writeable = no
guest ok = yes
printable = yes
```

Hybrid print shares can be configured to support other functions when used in conjunction with the print command parameter (see below) and printer input filters like smbprint (also below). For example, faxing can be incorporated as a network print function using tools like *HylaFAX* and *mgetty+sendfax*. Other options include setting up raw print shares for graphics. See the Faxing.txt and Printing.txt distribution documents for more information.

HylaFAX: http://www.hylafax.org
mgetty+sendfax: http://alpha.greenie.net/mgetty/

[printers] Share

Samba provides a simple mechanism for making all the printers identified in the UNIX printer configuration file available for use. The [printers] share is a special smb.conf section similar to the [homes] share discussed in Chapter 11. When an SMB connection setup request is received by the server, Samba first scans smb.conf, attempting to match the request to one of the specifically named shares. If a match is not found, it will then scan the passwd database, attempting to locate a match based on the client user name. If no match is found and a [printers] share is defined in the configuration file, it will then scan the UNIX printer configuration file to find a match. If a printer name match is found, Samba grants access to a temporary [*printer name*] share created by cloning the [printers] section definitions. A sample [printers] share is listed in Example 12.1.

Example 12.1   *Sample [printers] Share*

```
[printers]
        path = /var/spool/samba
        writeable = no
        guest ok = yes
        printable = yes
```

Share Level Parameters

Samba provides a set of additional share parameters that allow you further to tailor the behavior of individual print shares (Table 12.1). Most of these parameters involve specifying command scripts that will be used to query and manage the local UNIX print queues from Windows and LAN Manager clients. Default values are supplied for *some* of the command parameters based on the operating system type specified by the **printing** parameter.

Table 12.1   *Print Share Parameters*

print command	Print file handling command or script. Use %s or %f.
lpq command	Query print queue. User %p (printer).

continued on next page

Table 12.1 *continued*

lpq cache time	How long lpq info is cached; limits server load from repeated query requests from Windows clients. Default is 10 seconds. The Windows spool manager on each client will query a remote print queue every 15 seconds. The cache files are stored in /tmp/lpq.xxxx where xxxx is a hash of the lpq command in use.
lprm command	Remove a print job from a queue. Use %p (printer) and %j (job #).
lppause command	Pause a specific print job. Use %p (printer) and %j (job #).
lpresume command	Resume a specific print job. Use %p (printer) and %j (job #).
postscript	Force printing in postscript mode; fixes leading ctl-d problem by adding a %! sequence to the beginning of the file before sending it to the printer.
queuepause command	Pause a specific print queue. Use %p (printer).
queueresume command	Resume a specific print queue. Use %p (printer)

Print Command

In particular, you'll want to verify the options specified by the print command parameter. The value of print command is a text string that will be invoked via a system() call to process a print file after the file has been written to the spool directory. In general, this will result in the file's being handed off to the printing subsystem. The print command must remove the print file from the spool directory when processing has been completed. Example 12.2 displays print command defaults for the supported operating system types.

Example 12.2   *Default Print Command Values*

```
print command = lpr -r -P%p %s          AIX, BSD, LPRNG, PLP, QNX
print command = lp -c -d%p %s; rm %s     HPUX, SYSV
print command = lp -d%p -s %s; rm %s     SOFTQ
```

Note that the specified command must indicate the spool file name and, optionally, the printer name (Table 12.2). In addition, if guest ok is specified for the printer, some systems experience print failures if the guest account value is *nobody*. In this event, use an alternate UNIX account in the guest account parameter.

Command Parameter Scripts

The print command parameters listed in Table 12.1 designate a text string that represents any valid UNIX command or shell script combination. The parameter string value is passed to C library system( ) routine which then forks and executes sh (command language interpreter) to parse and execute the passed string. The command string value will likely include instances of Samba *substitution variables* (Table 12.2). Variable values will be resolved before passing the string to the system( ) routine. It is a good idea to use the full path name for any command or script in a command parameter value. This avoids problems associated resolving paths during execution. Sample command strings are listed in Example 12.3.

Table 12.2   *Printer Share Substitution Variables*

```
%p     printer name
%j     integer job number
%s     spool file name
%f     spool file name without full path prefix
```

Example 12.3 *Sample Command Strings*

AIX, BSD, LPRNG, PLP, QNX

```
lpq command = lpq %p

lprm command = lprm -P%p %j
```

HPUX, SYSV

```
lpq command = lpstat -o%p

lprm command = cancel %p-%j
```

Windows Client Setup

To setup access to a Samba managed printer on a Windows client from the desktop, select **Start → Settings → Control Panel → Printers → Add Printer** (Figure 12.1). From the displayed options, check **Network Printer** (Figure 12.2). Next, identify the server NetBIOS name and the printer name. You can use the browse tab to select a printer from the browse list if the printer is set **browseable** on the server (Figure 12.3). If the server has the target printer driver available for download and the client is a Windows 9x box, the driver will be automatically installed. After installation is complete, the Samba network printer can be used by applications just as if it were a local Windows print device.

Documents to be printed on the network device are routed to Samba by the Windows network redirector. Assuming the server has correctly configured the set of `print queue command` parameters, the client should be able to view and interact with the remote queue using the Windows spooling interface (Figure 12.4).

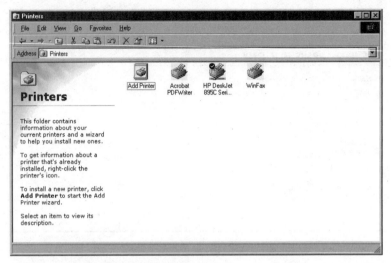

Figure 12.1 *Add a Printer panel*

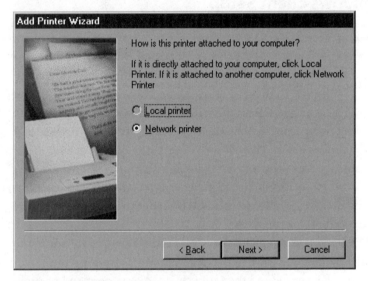

Figure 12.2 *Network Printer option*

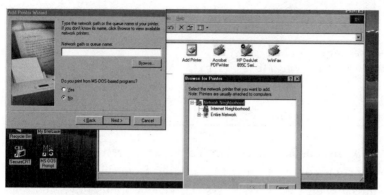

Figure 12.3   *Select server and printer name*

Document Name	Status	Owner	Progress	Started At
Microsoft Word - RFPstfc99-00....	Printing	DEROEST	0 bytes of 2....	9:47:10 AM 10/28/99
Microsoft Word - RFPstfc99-00....	Printing	deroest	0 of 5 pages	9:46:48 AM 10/28/99

HP DeskJet 895C Series Printer

Printer   Document   View   Help

2 jobs in queue

Figure 12.4   *Windows spool listing*

Windows 9x Drivers

Windows 9x boxes have a nice feature that allows them to download a
print driver from a server when adding a network printer. Samba supports the Windows 9x downloadable drivers feature via setting up a
share to hold the driver files, identifying a supported driver definition
file, `printers.def`, with the global `printer driver file` parameter, and then identifying the individual driver required for each print
share with the `printer driver`, and `printer driver location`
parameters.

To enable downloadable driver support, begin by creating a share
named [`printer$`]. Don't confuse this with the special [printers]
section (note the use of "**$**" instead of "**s**" in the share names). The
share should identify a directory with the `path` parameter that will
hold the driver files (Example 12.4).

Example 12.4   *Windows 9x Driver Share*

```
[printer$]
        path=/usr/local/samba/printer
        public=yes
        writeable=no
        browseable=yes
```

A driver definition file, `printers.def`, is created by first obtaining copies of the `msprint*.inf` files from the `\Windows\inf` directory on a Windows 9x system. Vendor printer drivers not supplied in the default `msprint*.inf` files will first need to be installed on a Windows 9x system. These will show up as some rendition of `oem*.inf` files in the `\Windows\inf` directory. Extract driver information from the `*.inf` files and append it to the Samba `printers.def` file by invoking the `make_printerdef` command. Supply a `.inf` file name and a specific driver name (enclosed in double quotes) as arguments to the command. Note that the supplied driver name must exactly match the vendor-supplied driver name expected by the Windows 9x client. Append `make_printerdef stdout` to the `printers.def` file (Example 12.5). A set of driver and dynamic link library (DLL) files will be output to `stderr`. These files can be found in the `\Windows\System` directory on a Windows 9x system and will need to be stored in the `[printers$]` driver directory.

Example 12.5   *Creating a Windows 9x Driver Definition*

```
make_printerdef msprint.inf "Apple LaserWriter" >> printers.def
```

Next identify the location of the drivers definition file by using the global `printer driver file` parameter. The default location is `/usr/local/samba/lib/printers.def`.

```
printer driver file = /usr/local/samba/lib/printers.def
```

Finally, add the `printer driver` and `printer driver location` parameters to each print share that will provide a downloadable driver (Example 12.6). The %h variable used with the printer driver location parameter will be replaced with the server name that Samba is running on. For more information on Windows 9x downloadable drivers, see PRINTER_DRIVER.txt file in the Samba distribution documentation.

Example 12.6   *Print Share with Downloadable Driver*

```
[LaserWriter]
        comment = Apple LaserWriter plus Driver
        browseable = yes
        printable = yes
        guest ok = yes
        writeable = no
        printer driver=Apple LaserWriter
        printer driver location=\\%h\PRINTER$
```

Windows Printers

Samba also supports UNIX printing to remote Windows printers via a spooling input filter, smbprint. The smbprint filter is basically a script wrapper for the smbclient command. smbprint pipes input into smbclient, which handles the connect session with the remote Windows spooling service. Two versions of the smbprint script are provided, smbprint (BSD) and smbprint.sysv (SYSV). The scripts are located in the Samba distribution subdirectory ./examples/printing.

smbprint (BSD)

To enable access to Windows-managed printers from a BSD UNIX system, begin by installing the smbprint script into the Samba binary directory. Create an /etc/printcap entry for the remote Windows printer similar to Example 12.7. Select a printer name, one or more aliases, and a spooling directory location. Create the spool directory per the location identified by the /etc/printcap :sd option for the new network printer entry.

Example 12.7   *BSD smbprint printcap Entry*

```
<printer name>: <printer alias>: \
    :cm=<printer description> \
    :sd=/var/spool/lpd\<printer name> \
    :af=/var/spool/lpd\<printer name>/<accounting file> \
    :if=/usr/local/samba/bin/smbprint \
    :mx=0 \
    :lp=/dev/null
```

Within the designated printer spool directory create a file named **.config** which will be used by the **smbprint** script to identify the remote *server*, *service*, and *password* (Example 12.8).

Example 12.8   */var/spool/samba/<printer name>/.config*

```
server=<server NetBIOS name>
service=<printer name>
password="<printer share password>"
```

Start the printer and validate access. smbprint will log activity messages to /tmp/smb-print.log. This file is quite useful for con-figuration debugging and testing. When you are certain the config-uration is working as expected, edit the smbprint script and set the logfile parameter to /dev/null.

```
logfile=/tmp/smb-print.log
```

smbprint (SYSV)

To use smbprint in an SYSV environment, copy smbprint.sys into the Samba install directory as file name smbprint. Edit the script and set the server, service, and password parameters for the remote Windows print service as with the BSD version. Note that under SYSV this information is included in the script rather than in a separate .config file. Next, invoke the lpadmin command to create a new interface for the printer in the printer administration directory (/etc/lp or /usr/lib/lp). The new interface will be used by lp to route jobs to the remote service. Finally, enable the printer and set it to accept jobs.

```
$ lpadmin -p<printer name> -v/dev/null -i/usr/local/samba/smbprint
```

```
$ enable printername
```

```
$ accept printername
```

Debugging Print Shares

To debug a print share:

- Verify that the printer name is a valid entry in the printer configuration file with the testprns command:

  ```
  $ testprns <printer name> <printcap file>
  ```

- Try setting the print command parameter to do a simple cp of the incoming print file into a temporary file. You can then verify the output using and editor:

  ```
  print command = cp %s /tmp/print.tmp
  ```

- Make sure /dev/null is world writeable. Samba uses /dev/null to discard messages and extraneous output from the designated print command.
- Make sure that all the commands and scripts used in the various printer command parameters include absolute path names or are in Samba's $PATH environment.
- Check for problems in the /etc/printcap definition.
- Try connecting to the printer using smbclient. Once you have successfully connected, try printing a file:

  ```
  smbclient '\\server\printer' -P
  ```

Summary

- To set up Samba as a print server begin by setting the printing, printcap name, and load printers parameters to define the operating system type, identify the printer configuration file, and indicate whether you would like all printers added to the browse list:

```
Printing = <os type>
Printcap name = <printer configuration file>
Load printers = <yes, no>
```

- Print shares can be defined either by a share name enclosed in square brackets or by using the special [printers] share section.

```
[print share name]
comment = <text description>
printer = <printcap printer name>
path = <spooling directory>
writeable = no
guest ok = yes
printable = yes
```

- The special [printers] share section represents the set of printer names listed in the printer configuration database identified by the printcap name parameter. The list is searched for a match using the client supplied printer name. If a match is found, a temporary share is set up using the matched name by cloning the parameters defined in the [printers] share.

- Share-level parameters include the definition of command scripts to be executed when printing or interacting with a print queue from a remote client. Command scripts are strings that represent any valid UNIX command or script:

```
print command = lpr -r -P%p %s
lpq command = lpq %p
lprm command = lprm -P%p %j
```

- A set of substitution variables is provided to identify the printer name, spool file name, and job number:

```
%p      printer name
%j      integer job number
%s      spool file name
%f      spool file name without full path prefix
```

- Windows 9x downloadable drivers are supported via a special share name [printer$] and a set of parameters identifying the driver directory location and driver name. The driver files are copied from the Windows. The driver definition file, printers.def is created from the Windows .inf files by the make_printerdef command.

Driver Share

```
[printer$]
  path=/usr/local/samba/printer
  public=yes
  writeable=no
  browseable=yes
```

Parameters

```
printer driver file = <printers.def path>

printer driver = <driver name>
printer driver location = <driver path>
```

Update printers.def

```
make_printerdef <.inf file> "<name>" >> printers.def
```

- UNIX printing to Windows printers is facilitated by Samba using printer input filters. Two filters are provided, smbprint (BSD) and smbprint.sysv (SYSV), that direct input to the smbclient command.

Part 04

Using Samba

13

Samba Clients

"On the other hand, you have different fingers."

Anonymous

Thus far in the text we have focused on Samba's role as a CIFS/SMB server. On one hand, Samba is a CIFS/SMB server, but on the other, it is also a CIFS/SMB client. In this chapter we'll look at how Samba can facilitate UNIX client access to shares managed by Windows as well as other Samba servers. We'll also review Windows client setup and CIFS/SMB options for other non-Windows platforms.

UNIX Client

Samba is not a CIFS/SMB one-way street. Along with its role as a CIFS/SMB server, Samba also provides UNIX client access to remote shares via its `smbclient`, `smbwrapper`, `smbtar`, and `smbprint` applications.

smbclient

smbclient is an extremely useful tool for testing Samba and Windows server configurations. In essence, **smbclient** is an *ftp-like* CIFS/SMB command line client application. Capabilities include moving files to and from file shares, creating and removing files and directories, printing files on remote printers, and exercising NetBIOS name-to-address resolution.

As you might imagine, a wide range of features also leads to a wide range of command parameters. It turns out that the parameter set is larger than we might think. What follows is a synopsis of available `smbclient` parameters and a few commonly used examples (Example 13.1).

When experimenting with the following parameters, keep in mind that Samba must interact with a wide range of CIFS/SMB platforms. This means varying degrees of protocol compliance. Some platforms can be a bit stubborn when it comes to parameter combinations and character case. If at first you don't succeed, try repeating the request using uppercased user names, passwords, NetBIOS names, and service names.

```
smbclient <service name> [password] [-s smb.conf path] [-B IP addr] \
[-O socket options][-R name resolve order] [-M NetBIOS name] \
[-i scope] [-N] [-n NetBIOS name] [-d debu glevel] [-P] [-p port] \
```

```
[-1 log base name] [-h] [-I dest IP] [-E] [-U user name] \
[-L NetBIOS name] [-t terminal code] [-m max protocol] \
[-W workgroup] [-T c|x IXFqgbNan] [-D directory] [-c command string]
```

smbclient Options

- *Service Name* represents the full NetBIOS name of the requested service, **\\server\share**. Note that UNIX uses the backslash character as an escape. That means you'll need to quote the service name string or use double backslashes, **'\\server\share'** or **\\\\server\\share**. An alternative is to use the Universal Network Convention (UNC) format, which substitutes a forward slash in place of a backslash, **//server/share**.

- *Password* is the access password for the service. The password can also follow the user name if the **-U** option is used. If a password is supplied, smbclient assumes a **-N** suppress option. If a password is required and not supplied on the command line, the client will prompt for a password during connection processing.

- **-s** *smb.conf path* indicates an alternate path name for the Samba configuration file.

- **-B** *IP addr* specifies the broadcast address for a NetBIOS name service request.

- **-O** *socket options* lists the set of TCP socket options to be used on the client socket. The set of supported socket options is listed in the smb.conf (5) man page. The syntax is *option=value*. Any options used should correspond to those supported by the operating system.

- **-R** *name resolve order* designates the order in which the various name service resources will be queried in order to resolve a NetBIOS name to network address. Options include **lmhosts** (check lmhosts file), **hosts** (check DNS, NIS or /etc/hosts), **wins** (check WINS), and **bcast** (broadcast query).

- **-M** *NetBIOS name* allows you to send a WinPopup message to the designated server. The message text can be piped into smb-client or entered interactively after a connection is established. Enter a control-d to terminate and send the message.

- **-i** *scope* identifies the NetBIOS scope to be used when generating NetBIOS names. The option is rarely used.

- **-N** will inhibit prompting for a password. This is useful when the target service does not require an access password. The option is assumed if a password was supplied on the command line.

- **-n** *NetBIOS name* indicates an alternative NetBIOS name for the local machine. If it is not supplied, smbclient will use the local machine's host name.

- **-d** *debug level* sets the value, 0-10 or "A," to indicate the verbosity of messages and warnings for debugging purposes. The higher the value, the more output. If the level is set to a value of "A," all output messages will be printed. The default value is "0."

- **-P** indicates that the target service should be treated as a printer. This option is no longer used in Samba version 2.0 and newer.

- **-p** *port* is used to indicate an alternate server TCP port number. The default well-known port number for a CIFS/SMB server is 139.

- **-l** *log base name* indicates the base text string to be used for the activity log. The default is specified at compile time.

- **-h** requests display of the usage information for **smbclient**.

- **-I** *dest IP* indicates the destination IP address of the target server ID dotted decimal form. Use of this option circumvents a name service lookup.

- **-E** reroutes messages from **stdout** to **stderr**.

- **-U** *user name* identifies the user name that will used when accessing the service. If it is not supplied, smbclient will assume the value indicated by the **USER** or **LOGNAME** environment variables. When the user name can't be resolved by these means it will default to a value of "**GUEST**." If the user name contains a "%" character, everything to the right of the character will be used as a password.

```
-U username%password
```

- **-L** *NetBIOS name* will request a list of shares available on the designated server.

- **-t** *terminal code* tells smbclient how to interpret file names on the target server. This is required to map between UNIX and Windows multibyte language representations. Supported terminal codes include **sjis, euc, jis7, jis8, junet, hex,** and **cap.** Check the source code for additional types.

* **-m** *max protocol level* is a pre-Samba 2.0 option that indicated the protocol level to be negotiated with the target server.

* **-W** *workgroup* set workgroup name to be used for the connection.

* **-T c|x IXFqgbNan** indicates the **tar** options to be used in creating a **tar** archive of a CIFS/SMB file share using **smbclient.**

Options

- **c**—Create an archive using the specified *file name*, *device*, or *stdout*. If using *stdout*, set debug level to "0." The "c" option is mutually exclusive with the "x" argument.

- **x**—Extract files from the *archive file*, *device*, or *stdin* and restore them to the file share. Files are restored into the top-level directory unless overridden with the **-D** option. File creation time will be set to the archive date saved.

- **I**— Include list of files and directories.

- **X**—Exclude list of files and directories

- **b**—Designate write block size * TBLOCK (set at compile time, usually 512 bytes).

- **g**—Include files that have the archive bit set.

- **q**— Specify quiet mode (no diagnostic messages).

- **r**—Include or exclude files based on regular expression matching.

- **N**— Include files newer than the indicated file.

- **a**—This resets the archive bit when a file is added to the archive.

- **-D** *directory* set the initial directory location.

- **-c** *command string* is a semicolon separated list of commands to be executed.

smbclient Interactive Mode Commands

When smbclient has connected and authenticated with the service the user is presented with a command prompt.

```
smb:\>
```

Once the prompt is displayed, you can interact with the service using the following list of commands. Interactive behavior is similar to FTP. Commands are case-insensitive single words that may be followed by one or more space-delimited arguments.

- **?** *[command]* Display help information for the indicated command. If a command is not specified, a list of available commands will be displayed.
- **!** *[shell command]* This will temporarily escape back to the UNIX shell. If a command is specified, it will be executed on the local machine.
- **cd** *[directory name]* This will change the working directory on the server to the indicated location. If no directory name is specified, the current working directory name is displayed.
- **del** *<mask>* Delete all files that match the specified "mask."
- **dir** *<mask>* List all files in the working directory that match the specified "mask."
- **exit** Terminate the server connection and exit **smbclient**.
- **get** *<remote file name>* *[local file name]* Copy the specified remote file from the server to the local system. If the "local file name" option is given, then rename the file using the designated name. No content translations are performed (binary mode transfer).
- **help** *[command]* See **?**[command] above.
- **lcd** *[directory name]* Change the local working directory to the specified "directory name." If a directory name is not specified, the name of the current local working directory is displayed.
- **lowercase** Toggles whether file names copied by a **get** or **mget** command are converted to lower case (ON by default).
- **ls** *<mask>* See the `dir` command above.
- **mask** *<mask>* Defines a file name match pattern that will be used with recursive **mget** and **mput** operations. For example, a mask of "`*.c`" would collect all C source files from the directory tree.
- **md** *<directory name>* See the **mkdir** command.
- **mget** *<mask>* Copy all files matching the mask pattern from the remote file share to the local working directory. Note that the mask is interpreted differently during recursive operation (see **mask** and **recurse** commands).

- **mkdir** *<directory name>* Create the specified directory name on the server file share.
- **mput** *<mask>* Copy all files matching mask pattern from the local working directory to the working directory on the remote file share. Note that the mask is interpreted differently during recursive operation (see **mask** and **recurse** commands).
- **print** *<file name>* Print the specified local file to a printable service on the remote server per print mode settings.
- **printmode** *<graphics or text>* Set the print mode to graphics (binary) or text.
- **prompt** Toggle **mget** and **mput** prompting for filenames during file copy processing.
- **put** *<local file name>* *[remote file name]* Copy the specified file from the local system to the remote server file share. If the "remote file name" option is given, then rename the file using the designated name. No content translations are performed (binary mode transfer).
- **queue** Display print queue jobs by ID, name, size, and status.
- **quit** See the **exit** command.
- **rd** *<directory name>* See the **rmdir** command.
- **recurse** Toggle **mput** and **mget** directory recursion. When toggled on, these commands will walk the source directory tree collecting files that match the **mask** pattern. See also the **mask** command.
- **rm** *<mask>* Remove files that match the mask pattern from the current working directory on the server file share.
- **rmdir** *<directory name>* Remove the specified directory from the server file share.
- **tar c|x [IXbgNa]** Create or extract a tar archive. See the **-T** command line option above. See also **blocksize** and **tarmode** commands.
- **blocksize** *<blocksize>* Causes the **tar** file to be written out per the specified *blocksize* multiplied by TBLOCK (TBLOCK is set a compile time, default 512).
- **tarmode** <full|inc|reset|noreset> Sets tar behavior per file archive bit settings.
- **full**—all files added to archive.
- **inc**—only include files with archive bit set.

- **reset**—reset the archive bit after adding to archive.
- **noreset**—don't reset archive bit after adding to archive.
- **setmode** *<filename>* **<perm=[+ | \-]rsha>** Set DOS file permissions. Similar to DOS `attrib` command.
  - **r**—readonly
  - **s**—system
  - **h**—hidden
  - **a**—archive

Example 13.1   *smbclient Examples*

List shares

```
$ smbclient  -L wizard -N
```

Send a message

```
$ echo 'Samba down for maintenance' | smbclient -M wizard
```

Make a backup

```
$ smbclient //wizard/C "" -N -Tc archive.tar
```

Query a print queue

```
$ smbclient //wizard/hplaser -c queue
```

---

smbwrapper

Samba doesn't natively support mounting CIFS/SMB file shares on a UNIX client. There is some support for mounted file shares with operating system-specific implementations like Linux `smbfs`. What Samba does offer is an experimental tool called `smbwrapper` that allows UNIX clients limited file operations on CIFS/SMB services.

`smbwrapper` exploits a capability in some UNIX implementations that support dynamic loading of shared libraries. It is based on a loadable library, `smbwrapper.so`, that distinguishes between CIFS/SMB file operations and standard UNIX file operations. As of this writing the code has been tested on the following operating systems: Linux 2.0 with glibc2 (RH5.1), Linux 2.1 with glibc2, Solaris

2.5.1 with gcc, Solaris 2.6 with gcc, SunOS 4.1.3 with gcc, IRIX 6.4 with cc, and OSF1 with gcc.

If you are interested in experimenting with the code under another UNIX implementation that supports loadable shared libraries, refer to the **Readme** and **Porting** documents in the distribution ./source/smbwrapper directory.

UNIX commands that have been successfully tested against remote CIFS/SMB service include: emacs, tar, ls, cmp, cp, rsync, du, cat, rm, mv, less, more, wc, head, tail, bash, tcsh, mkdir, rmdir, vim, xedit, and diff.

smbwrapper is not installed by default. In order to build and install the code, change directory to the ./source/smbwrapper directory in the Samba source distribution tree and type, **make smbwrapper**.

```
$ make smbwrapper
```

Once this is built and installed, initiate an smbwrapper subshell by invoking the smbsh command. smbsh will prompt you for a user name and password (Example 13.2). The user name and password is sent to any server supporting *user-level security*.

Example 13.2 *smbsh Session*

```
$ smbsh
Username: <user name>
Password: <password>
```

Within the smbsh subshell, you can interact with CIFS/SMB servers by specifying a path name that is rooted with the special directory name /smb and followed with a *server name* and *service*. The /smb root lets the smbsh subshell know that you are requesting access to an SMB service versus a local file or directory resource (Example 13.3).

```
/smb/<server>/<service>
```

Example 13.3 *List Services on Remote SMB Server*

```
$ ls /smb/wizard
smbtar
```

Another method for interacting with remote CIFS/SMB file shares is provided by the smbtar script. This is a wrapper script for smbclient that simplifies using smbclient's tar options. You can use smbtar to backup and restore files residing on a remote file share (Example 13.4). The target file share may reside under a Windows platform or under another Samba server. smbtar can also be incorporated into UNIX shell scripts to automate backup operations using timed batch services like cron.

Example 13.4   *smbtar - Dump & Restore*

Incremental Dump

```
smbtar -s <NetBIOS name> -p <password> -x <Share Name> \
<device> -I
```

Restore Share

```
smbtar -s <NetBIOS name> -p <password> -x <Share Name> \
<device> -r
```

smbprint

Samba supports UNIX client printing to remote Windows printers via a spooling input filter, **smbprint**. The **smbprint** filter is another script wrapper for the smbclient command. **smbprint** pipes input into **smbclient** which handles the connect session with the remote Windows spooling service. Two versions of the **smbprint** script are provided, smbprint (BSD) and smbprint.sysv (SYSV). The scripts are located in the Samba distribution subdirectory ./examples/printing. Refer to the "Windows Printers" section of Chapter 12 for details on using the **smbprint** interface.

Windows 9x and Windows NT

In the preceding chapters, I discussed Windows client configuration as it related to the various CIFS/SMB services provided by Samba. I'll briefly cover the basics of Windows client configuration again here, but will refer you to those chapters that specifically address topics like NetBIOS over TCP, name service, workgroups, and domains for detailed information. I'll illustrate Windows 9x setup because Windows NT platforms are quite similar.

To set up a Windows 9x computer as a workgroup or domain member, begin by verifying that the TCP protocol is installed and that NetBIOS over TCP support is enabled. Click **Start →Settings → Control Panel → Network**. Locate or add TCP/IP for your network adapter and select the **NetBIOS** tab from the TCP/IP properties panel (Figure 13.1).

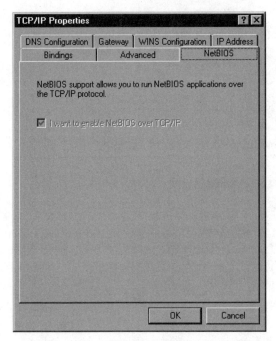

Figure 13.1   *Windows 9x TCP NetBIOS panel*

If WINS will be used for NetBIOS name service, select the **WINS Configuration** tab and identify one or more WINS servers (Figure 13.2)

Before rebooting, specify the computer's NetBIOS name and workgroup name by selecting **Identification** tab from the **Network** panel (Figure 13.3). The system will update the registry and reboot after exiting the Identification panel.

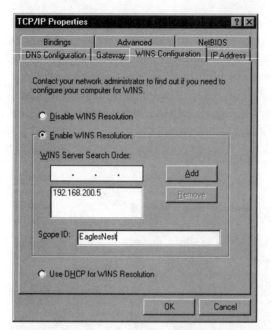

Figure 13.2   Windows 9x WINS server identification

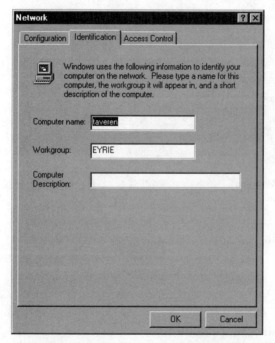

Figure 13.3   Windows 9x NetBIOS name panel

Last, if the computer will be a member of a domain, enable domain logons by selecting **Start → Settings → Control Panel → Network** from the desktop. Make sure that Client for Microsoft Networks is installed. Highlight **Client for Microsoft Networks** and select the **properties** tab. Set the **Logon to Windows NT** domain box and enter the name of the domain (Figure 13.4). Apply the changes and restart. The **Windows Logon** box should now display *user*, *password*, and *domain* options. The first time each user logs on to the domain he/she will be asked about saving the user profile. The user should select **Yes**. Check the Samba roaming profiles store to verify that a profile was created for the new user.

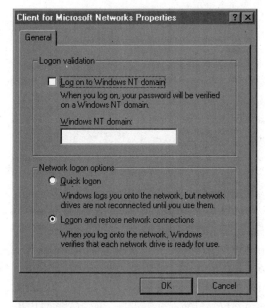

Figure 13.4   *Client for Microsoft Networks Properties*

DOS and Windows 3.x Clients

There are a number of options for including DOS and older Windows systems as members of your Samba workgroup or domain. For DOS and Windows 3.x systems, you can obtain free copies of either Microsoft Network Client for DOS or Microsoft

LAN Manager Client for DOS from the Microsoft ftp sites listed below. Download and execute the self-extracting disk images. Installation documentation is included in the archives.

ftp://ftp.microsoft.com/BusSys/Clients/MSCLIENT/
ftp://ftp.microsoft.com/BusSys/Clients/LANMAN/

Other options include Digital Pathworks Client for DOS, IBM LAN Client for DOS, and IBM DOS LAN Requester.

Windows for Workgroups platforms will need to have the TCP/IP stack installed. You can download a free copy from the following Microsoft ftp site.

ftp://ftp.microsoft.com/BusSys/Clients/WFW/

OS/2

Just as with MS Windows, there are many versions of OS/2 available, so for sake of brevity we'll focus on one, OS/2 Warp. OS/2 Warp Version 4 supports NetBEUI over TCP/IP via its peer-to-peer networking services. To include OS/2 workstations in a workgroup or domain, begin by verifying or adding NetBIOS over TCP/IP to the set of network protocols. From the OS/2 desktop, run the IBM *Multi-Protocol Transport Services (MPTS)* configuration program and select **Adapters and Protocol Services → Configure → LAN Adapters and Protocols** respectively to display the **Adapter and Protocol Configuration** menu (Figure 13.5). If it is not already installed, add **IBM OS/2 NETBIOS OVER TCP/IP** protocol. Before rebooting the system you'll need to edit the **\IBM-LAN\IBMLAN.INI** file on the OS/2 boot drive. Check the **[networks]** section of the **IBMLAN.INI** file and verify that MPTS added an entry for **TCPBEUI$**. The stanzas should look something like Example 13.5. Add a **TCPBEUI$** entry if it is missing. Also verify that the **wrknets** and **srvnets** parameters refer to both the **NET1** and **NET2 [networks]** stanzas.

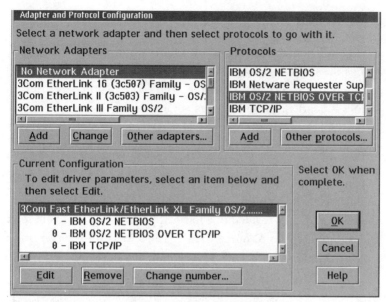

Figure 13.5   *Adapter and protocol configuration*

Example 13.5   *IBMLAN.INI Stanzas for NetBIOS over TCP/IP*

```
net1 = TCPBEUI$,0,LM10,100,150,14
net2 = NETBEUI$,0,LM10,100,150,14
        . . .
wrknets = NET1, NET2
        . . .
srvnets = NET1, NET2
```

Now you can reboot the machine. To finish up, you'll need to update the NetBIOS Name List and Broadcast List for name service by running MPTS configuration and selecting **Adapters and Protocol Services → Configure → LAN Adapters and Protocols**. Highlight **IBM OS/2 NETBIOS OVER TCP/IP** and select **Edit**. On the **NetBIOS over TCP/IP** panel, bring up the **Edit/Change** menus for the NetBIOS and broadcast lists. Finally, register the name list changes by invoking **\IBMCOM\RFCADDR**.

Macintosh

The DAVE toolkit distributed by Thursby Software Systems, Inc., brings the CIFS/SMB world onto the Macintosh desktop. DAVE implements all services defined by the CIFS protocol, as well as WINS support and Windows domain logins. A DAVE client can act as both CIFS/SMB client and CIFS/SMB server. Other features include support for WinPopup messages and network printing.

DAVE clients access CIFS/SMB services using the standard Macintosh chooser interface (Figure 13.6). From the chooser, users can interact with Windows workgroup and domain services just as they would if they resided in a local Appletalk network. Windows clients interact with resources residing on a Macintosh server using standard browse interfaces like Network Neighborhood.

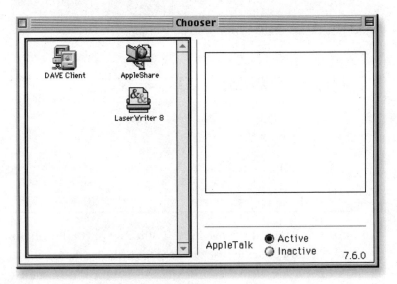

Figure 13.6   *DAVE CIFS/SMB chooser interface*

DAVE is compatible with Windows 9x, Windows NT and Windows 2000. For more information, refer to the Thursby Web page: **http://www.thursby.com**.

Summary

- Samba supports UNIX client access to remote CIFS/SMB servers via the `smbclient`, `smbwrapper`, `smbtar`, and `smbprint` routines.

- `smbclient` is an "ftp-like" CIFS/SMB command-line client application. Capabilities include moving files to and from file shares, creating and removing files and directories, printing files on remote printers and exercising NetBIOS name-to-address resolution.

  ```
  $ smbclient -L <server>
  ```

- `smbwrapper` is an experimental tool that allows UNIX clients limited file operations on CIFS/SMB file services. Uses a loadable, shared library invoked by `smbsh` subshell. It is not installed by default. See the distribution document `./source/smbwrapper/Readme`.

  ```
  $ smbsh
  ```

- `smbtar` is a wrapper script for `smbclient` that simplifies using `smbclient`'s `tar` options.

  ```
  $ smbtar -s <server> -c|x <chare> <device>
  ```

- `smbprint` is a printcap filter that pipes print input into `smbclient` for distribution to remote printer shares.

- Other CIFS/SMB clients include:
  - **Windows 9x, Windows NT:** Integrated NetBEUI over TCP/IP.
  - **DOS, Windows 3x, WWG:** MS Network Client, DOS LAN Manager, TCP/IP Stack:
    ftp://ftp.microsoft.com/ BusSys/Clients
  - OS/2 Warp: peer-to-peer networking
  - **Macintosh:** DAVE—Thursby Software Systems, Inc.; **http://www.thursby.com**

14

Administration Tools

Command line or GUI, that is the question.

Whether tis nobler in the mind to suffer

The slings and arrows of the UNIX command line

Or invoke a GUI admin tool against a sea of
configuration troubles.

Graphical interfaces seem to be the trend when it comes to administering complex software systems. The ubiquitous platform-independent nature of the Web has made browser-based administration tools the interfaces of choice. There are still a few of us who prefer the tried-and-true command-line approach to system administration. However, most system administrators will admit that GUI-based tools reduce the number of configuration errors in complex tables. They also assist new systems administrators in tailoring unfamiliar applications.

There is an ever-growing collection of GUI administration tools directed at simplifying Samba configuration and in this chapter we'll take a brief tour of some of them. Before we delve into the color-filled, form-based world of GUI tools, let's start with good old command-line tools.

Command-Line Tools

testparm

An excellent command-line tool for verifying general `smb.conf` correctness is the Samba `testparm` command. `testparm` will not guarantee that a particular share or section will operate the way you expect, rather it will validate the syntax and parameters you have specified for each section in the configuration file. Invoke `testparm` with the full path name of the target `smb.conf` file as an argument. If a host name or IP address is supplied as an option, it will also check the access rights of the specified host. See the `testparm` (1) man page for additional information.

```
$ testparm <-s configfilename> <hostname hostIP>
```

smbclient

We talked about using the `smbclient` command a number of times in the text to validate access to servers and services. `smbclient` can be used to move files between file shares, modify files and directories, print files on remote printers and exercise NetBIOS name-to-address resolution. Refer to Chapter 13 "Samba Clients" and the `smbclient` (1) man page for detailed information on `smbclient` options.

```
$ smbclient -L <server> -N
```

smbstatus

The smbstatus command is a simple tool that will display information about active connections to your server. Server status information can be limited to users, shares or locks. This is a useful tool for making a quick check on the general health of the server. See the smbstatus (1) man page for options and additional information.

```
$ smbstatus -d
testprns
```

Verify that the printer name is a valid entry in the printer configuration file with the testprns command. See the testprns (1) man page for more information.

```
$ testprns <printer name> <printcap file>
```

Web Tools

SWAT

For those more accustomed to the ease of use and error checking provided by a GUI configuration tool, Samba Version 2.x provides a Web-based configuration and administration tool aptly named the *Samba Web Administration Tool (SWAT)* (Figure 14.1). Being Web based, SWAT can be invoked from a remote networked workstation. This is a handy capability when you are administering a number of geographically disparate Samba servers or making those late-night configuration changes over a dialup link from the comfort of your home. SWAT provides HTML forms for the various section types represented in the smb.conf file (Figure 14.2). SWAT simplifies general configuration tasks and allows the system administrator to focus on the section definition of interest. Refer to Chapter 6 "Samba Configuration – smb.conf" and the swat (8) man page for details on installing and using SWAT.

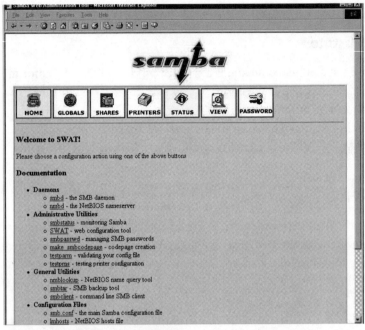

Figure 14.1   *Samba SWAT administration tool*

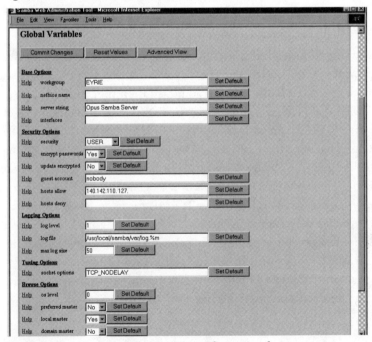

Figure 14.2   *Sample SWAT action configuration form*

Webmin

Webmin is another Web-based tool for administering Samba configuration. It goes much further than SWAT by supporting a wide range of general UNIX administration tasks (Figure 14.3). Using Webmin you can configure Samba, set up user accounts, manage DNS, and administer file systems, Web servers and more.

Webmin uses a set of Perl 5 CGI programs to update various UNIX configuration tables. The administrator interface requires browser support for forms, frames and Java. To obtain a copy of Webmin or additional information, visit the Webmin Web site: **http://www.webmin.com/webmin/**.

User	Modules	
admin	Scheduled Cron Jobs	BIND 4 DNS Server
	NFS Exports	Internet Services and Protocols
	Bootup and Shutdown Actions	Disk and Network Filesystems
	Samba Windows File Sharing	Users, Groups and Passwords
	Partitions on Local Disks	Running Processes
	Webmin Configuration	Disk Quotas
	Software Packages	PPP Usernames and Passwords
	Webmin Users	Apache Webserver
	Printer Administration	BIND 8 DNS Server
	Sendmail Configuration	Squid Proxy Server
	File Manager	Network Configuration
	DHCP Server	Majordomo List Manager
	Firewall Configuration	
jcameron	Scheduled Cron Jobs	Users, Groups and Passwords
	Apache Webserver	Sendmail Configuration

Create a new Webmin user.

Figure 14.3   *Webmin UNIX administration*

SMB2WWW

SMB2WWW is a tool that provides a Web interface to the Samba **smbclient** command. It presents a Network Neighborhood-like view of a workgroup or domain (Figure 14.4). Click on any server listed on the page and a list of available services is displayed. SMB2WWW allows you to do most of the operations provided by smbclient. This includes tar'ing a file share directory for backup and restore purposes. For more information try out the demo page or archive site listed below.

http://us3.samba.org/samba/smb2www/index.html
http://www.scintilla.utwente.nl/users/frank/smb2www/

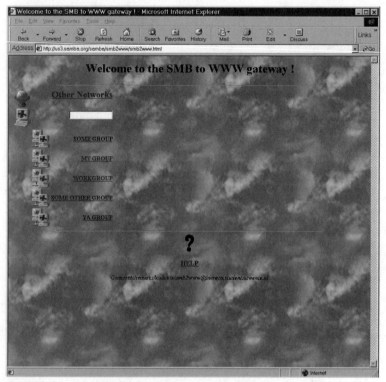

Figure 14.4　　SMB2WWW network neighborhood

Smbconftool

Smbconftool is another `smb.conf` editing tool. Unlike SWAT, smbconftool will preserve comments in `smb.conf`. However, you cannot enter comments. That capability will come in a future release. You can do most general configuration tasks like creating, updating, and removing share sections.

Smbconftool is Java-based, so will require Java support in the browser. You can obtain a copy of `smbconftool` from: **http://www.eatonweb.com/samba/**.

Windows Tools

bbSAT

The HP 3000 Channel Partner B+B Unternehmensberatung built a Windows-based GUI tool called bbSAT (Figure 14.5) for maintaining Samba configuration. This was done as part of the Samba port MPE/iX. bbSAT is freely available and will work with other Samba platforms. Like smbconftool, bbSAT will preserve **smb.conf** comments. There is also an enhanced version of bbSAT called "bbSAT (GE) Gold Edition" that provides additional functionality. For more information visit the bbSAT Web site: **http://jazz.external.hp.com/ src/samba/bbsat_index.html.**

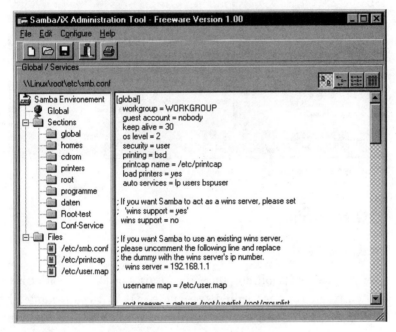

Figure 14.5 *bbSAT*

smbedit

smbedit is another free Win32 application for editing **smb.conf** from a Windows client (Figure 14.6). Along with general Samba configuration editing, you can also invoke Samba services like testparm and smbstatus. For more information see the smbedit Web page: **http://us3.samba.org/samba/smbedit/readme.htm.**

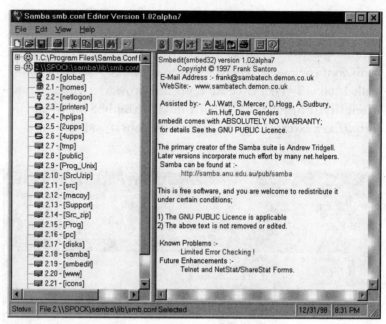

Figure 14.6   *smbedit*

Other Tools

smb-mode.el

For you Emacs aficionados, there is an Emacs major mode available for editing `smb.conf` called `smb-mode.el`. With smb-mode.el you can edit individual `smb.conf` sections, look up parameter information from the Samba man pages, perform parameter completion, and run a buffer through the Samba `testparm` command. To get a copy of smb-mode.el, look at the following Web site: **http://users.gtn.net/fraserm/smbmode.html**.

GSMB

Departing a bit from our focus on `smb.conf` editing tools, we note a Gtk tool for administering Samba `smbpasswd` encrypted password support called gsmb (Figure 14.7). It was created by Lauent Foucher. gsmb uses the Gtk 1.2.0 library. For more information visit the gsmb Web site: **http://savage.iut-blagnac.fr/projets/developpement/gsmb/**.

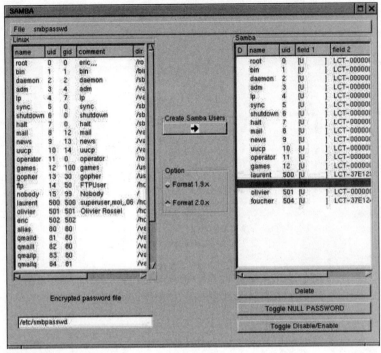

Figure 14.7   *gsmb*

Summary

- Useful Samba administration command line tools include: testparm, smbclient, smbstatus, and testprns.
- Useful Samba GUI administration tools include:
  - **Web Tools:** SWAT, Webmin, SMB2WWW, and smbconftool.
  - **Windows Tools:** bbSAT and smbedit.
  - **Other Tools:** smb-mode.el and gsmb.

Troubleshooting

"Politics is the art of looking for trouble, finding it, misdiagnosing it, and then misapplying the wrong remedies."

Groucho Marx

Computers are somewhat like politics. Sooner or later trouble always shows up. It usually happens when you're making one small late-night change to a production service. You know the kind. It's always some preventative service patch for a problem you've never seen; one the vendor advises needs to be applied, assuring that it is only a benign software update. You apply the patch and dream of sleeping in late the following morning. Just as you're ready to call it a night, problem symptoms start showing up from multiple subsystems. SNMP monitor alerts are popping up everywhere announcing server failures all across the network. In a nervous adrenalin rush you rapidly try to back out the patch before it's too late. Halfway through, the uninstall task fails, your screen goes blank, and the phone begins to ring off the hook.

Gruesome isn't it? You can't avoid computer and network problems, but you can limit the scope of disaster. The trick is to always have a good selection of diagnostic tools at hand, and to have a sound fallback plan. When installing a new system, try it out first in an isolated test environment. When problems emerge in production systems, address them as a series of validation stages. Begin with the lowest-level subsystems. In turn, examine each higher-level service eliminating possibilities as you proceed. This process will assist in diagnosing events rooted in complex subsystem interrelationships.

Sleuthing Samba

Samba is an excellent example of a network service comprised of tightly coupled subsystems. It is therefore often helpful to address Samba problems in the stepwise manner described in the previous paragraph. Begin by verifying network connectivity from both the server and client end of a circuit. Next confirm that the smbd and nmbd are running and listening for connection requests. Ensure that the configuration files correctly reflect the role Samba is playing in the workgroup or domain. When all else fails, make sure you know where to go for help.

In the following sections we'll look closely at validating Samba services at the network, daemon and configuration levels. Table 15.1 lists the set of tools we'll use as we analyze each component of the system.

Table 15.1 *Troubleshooting Tools*

Samba Tools

```
smbclient
nmblookup
testparm
testprns
```

UNIX Tools

```
ifconfig
netstat
ping
ps
iostat
```

Windows Client Tools

```
NET
NBTSTAT
WINIPCFG
```

Network Connectivity

Begin troubleshooting by examining network connectivity between clients and servers.

Can everybody talk to each other over the wire? Is everyone configured to support NetBIOS over TCP/IP? Are the assigned IP addresses and subnets correct? Use the `ifconfig` command on each UNIX client and server (Example 15.1) and the `winipcfg` command on Windows clients and servers (Figure 15.1) to verify network interface configuration. These commands will display adapter status, assigned IP address and subnet mask, and the broadcast address.

Example 15.1 *ifconfig – UNIX Network Interface*

```
# ifconfig en0
en0: flags=a080863<UP,BROADCAST,NOTRAILERS,RUNNING,SIMPLEX,
        MULTICAST,GROUPRT>
inet 145.142.210.20 netmask 0xffffff00 broadcast
    145.142.210.255
```

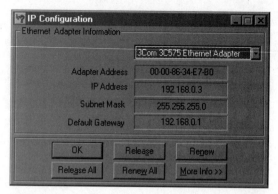

Figure 15.1   *winipcfg – Windows network interface*

Once you're certain that each systems network interface is operational, check reachability by using the **ping** command to send an ICMP echo request between problem systems (Example 15.2). Echo round-trip time and dropped-packet rate statistics are displayed, indicating the overall health of the communication path between the participating systems.

Example 15.2   *ping – Verify Communication Path*

```
# ping foo.bar.com
PING foo.bar.com (130.111.58.1): 56 data bytes
64 bytes from 130.111.58.1: icmp_seq=0 ttl=252 time=8 ms
64 bytes from 130.111.58.1: icmp_seq=1 ttl=252 time=3 ms
64 bytes from 130.111.58.1: icmp_seq=2 ttl=252 time=8 ms
64 bytes from 130.111.58.1: icmp_seq=3 ttl=252 time=5 ms
--- foo.bar.com ping statistics ---
4 packets transmitted, 4 packets received, 0% packet loss
round-trip min/avg/max = 3/5/8 ms
```

In most cases reachability problems will be related to routing configuration or an incorrectly assigned subnet mask. Use the netstat command to display additional interface statistics (Table 15.2) including netmask and routing information (Example 15.3). An interval flag may be used with netstat to collect statistics snapshots over time.

Table 15.2   *Useful netstat Options*

- i	Interface state, packet rates and errors.
- a	Display socket connection status.
- r	Display routing table information.
- m	Display memory allocation and usage (mbufs).

Example 15.3   *netstat – Display Routing*

```
$ netstat -rn
Routing tables
Destination    Gateway Flags    Refs    Use If  PMTU Exp Groups
Netmasks:
(0) 0 ff00
(0) 0 ffff ff00

Route Tree for Protocol Family 2:
default      145.142.210.100   UG 22    23884982   en0  -  -
127          127.0.0.1         U  3      637989     lo0  -  -
140.142.78   145.142.210.20    U  4      20262917   en0  -  -
```

Running Daemons

If you are confident that all network communication paths are functioning correctly, then the next step is to certify that the Samba smbd and nmbd daemons are running and listening for connections. Display the process status of smbd and nmbd with the ps command (Example 15.4).

Review inetd configuration (see "Configuration Files" section) to verify that the daemons will be spawned when SMB services are requested. Check the **smb.log** and **nmb.log** files in **/usr/local/samba/var** for diagnostic messages indicating any startup or communication anomalies.

Example 15.4   *'ps' Check Daemon Process Instance*

```
# ps -ef | grep smbd
root 448 1 0 07:25 ? 00:00:00 /usr/local/samba/bin/smbd -D

# ps -ef | grep nmbd
root 446 1 0 07:25 ? 00:00:00 /usr/local/samba/bin/nmbd -D
```

Assuming that the smbd and nmbd daemons are up and running, next look to see if they are listening for incoming connection requests. Invoke netstat with the -a option to list the set of port listening services on the server. You can thin the list down to just the NetBIOS services by piping the command into grep (Example 15.5).

Example 15.5   *Samba Listing to NetBIOS Ports*

```
$ netstat -a | grep netbios

tcp    0      0 *:netbios-ssn    ":"  LISTEN
udp    0      0 *:netbios-ns     ":"
udp    0      0 *:netbios-dgm    ":"
```

At this point we know that smbd and nmbd are up and listening for network requests. The question now is whether they will actually respond to a request. Verify responsiveness by sending a query to each daemon from local and remote clients.

Check smbd on the local server by executing the smbstatus and smbclient commands. The smbstatus command will display the server version, active connection list, lock file, and memory utilization statistics (Example 15.6). Use the -L option of the smbclient command to ask the server for a list of shares (Example 15.7). If smbd is responding, you should see output similar to the examples. If you experience password errors, verify that the security and encrypt passwords parameters are correct for your authentication environment. Also check for hosts allow, hosts deny, or valid users parameters that might restrict access.

Example 15.6   *smbstatus*

```
$ smbstatus -d

Samba version 2.0.5a
Service  uid   gid    pid      machine
--------------------------------------

No locked files

Share mode memory usage (bytes):
1048464(99%) free + 56(0%) used + 56(0%) overhead =
              1048576(100%) total
```

Example 15.7   *smbclient Share List*

```
$ smbclient -L BONZO

Domain=[LAB] OS=[Unix] Server=[Samba 2.1.0-prealpha]

    Sharename   Type   Comment
    ---------   ----   -------
    netlogon    Disk
    IPC$        IPC    IPC Service (UW Lab login)

    Server        Comment
    ------        -------
    BOZNO         Lab login server
    ZARDOZ        Presentation Workstation

    Workgroup     Master
    ---------     ------
    EYRIE         WIZARD
    TEST          ILLUSTRIOUS
    LAB           BONZO
```

Ask Samba for the same share list from a remote Windows client by invoking NET LIST from a command window.

```
NET VIEW \\<Samba \\<Samba NetBIOS name>
```

Now verify that **nmbd** is responding to queries both locally and from remote clients. From the local server execute the **nmblookup** command with the local host name as an argument. **nmbd** should respond with the server's IP address confirming that it is correctly handling name service queries (Example 15.8). You can further exercise **nmbd** by requesting a name list via broadcast (Example 15.9). Remember that if the workgroup or domain spans multiple subnets, you'll need one or more WINS servers to support cross-subnet name service.

Example 15.8   *nmbd Name Service Test*

```
# nmblookup -B OPUS __SAMBA__
Sending queries to 0.0.0.0
145.142.210.145 opus<00>
```

Example 15.9   *Name Query Broadcast*

```
# nmblookup -d 2 '*'
Added interface ip=145.142.210.145 bcast=145.142.210.255
nmask=255.255.255.0
Sending queries to 145.142.210.255
Got a positive name query response from 145.142.210.145 (
145.142.110.145 )
Got a positive name query response from 145.142.210.68 (
145.142.210.68 )
        ...
145.142.210.102 *<00>
145.142.210.227 *<00>
145.142.210.74 *<00>
```

The Windows NBTSTAT command is a good all-purpose tool for verifying NetBIOS over TCP services and statistics in a workgroup or domain (Table 15.3). You can use NBTSTAT to verify both smbd and nmbd information from Windows clients and servers (Example 15.10).

Table 15.3 *NBTSTAT – Options*

**NBTSTAT [-a <*RemoteName*>] [-A <*IP address*>] [-c] [-n] [-r] **
[-R] [-s] [S] [<*interval*>]]

–a	Lists the remote machine's name table given its name
–A	Lists the remote machine's name table given its IP address
–c	Lists the remote name cache including the IP addresses
–n	Lists local NetBIOS names
–r	Lists names resolved by broadcast and via WINS
–R	Purges and reloads the remote cache name table
–S	Lists sessions table with the destination IP addresses
–s	Lists sessions table converting destination IP addresses to host names via the hosts file

Example 15.10 *NBTSTAT*

```
C:\ NBTSTAT -c WIZARD

Node IpAddress: [192.168.0.2] Scope Id:[]
        NetBIOS Remote Cache Name Table

        Name    Type    Host Address   Life [sec]
        -----------------------------------------
        WIZARD  <00>    UNIQUE  192.168.0.1   360

C:\ NBTSTAT -a WIZARD

        NetBIOS Remote Machine Name Table

        Name            Type            Status
        - - - - - - - - - - - - - - - - - - - - - - - - - - -
        WIZARD          <00> UNIQUE     Registered
        EYRIE           <00> GROUP      Registered
        WIZARD          <03> UNIQUE     Registered
        WIZARD          <20> UNIQUE     Registered
        EYRIE           <1E> GROUP      Registered
        DEROEST         <03> UNIQUE     Registered
        EYRIE           <1D> UNIQUE     Registered
        .._MSBROWSE__..<01> GROUP       Registered
```

Configuration Files

Startup

If you discovered by means of a `ps` process check, that one or both of the Samba `smbd` and `nmbd` daemons weren't running verify that your daemon startup configuration is correct. Remember that the Samba daemons may be started either as persistent processes by `init` during system initialization or automatically when a service request is received by `inetd` (Example 15.11).

Example 15.11   *Samba Daemon Startup Configuration*

```
init boot-time startup - /etc/rc<file>

/usr/local/samba/bin/smbd -D
/usr/local/samba/bin/nmbd -D

   -or-

inetd service startup - /etc/inetd.conf

netbios-ssn stream tcp nowait root /usr/sbin/tcpd \
            /usr/local/samba/bin/smbd smbd
netbios-ns dgram udp wait root /usr/sbin/tcpd \
            /usr/local/samba/bin/nmbd nmbd
```

Service Ports

Server connection problems may be related to missing or invalid port numbers in `/etc/services`. Make sure that `udp port 137` and `tcp port 139` are reserved by the `netbios-ns` and `netbios-ssn` services respectively (Example 15.12).

Example 15.12   *Samba Port Configuration*

```
/etc/services

netbios-ns      137/udp
netbios-ssn     139/tcp
```

smb.conf

Overall behavior of Samba is proscribed by the `smb.conf` file. The *global section* of `smb.conf` should include parameters that identify the server's NetBIOS name, the workgroup/domain name, the security type, and whether passwords will be encrypted or in plain text (Table 15.4).

Table 15.4   *Important Global Section Parameters*

```
security = <share, user, server, domain>
netbios name = <server NetBIOS name>
workgroup = <workgroup/domain name>
password server = < >
encrypt passwords = true
```

Next check the parameters that identify Samba's role in services like WINS, browsing and domains. Refer to the chapters regarding each of these services in order to confirm whether Samba is acting as a client or server.

Verify that access control parameters in the global and service sections of `smb.conf` are reflecting the desired access permissions for the server and each share. For example, you may be blocking access due to improperly configured `hosts allow` and `hosts deny` parameters.

The `smb.conf` file can become unwieldy for complex sites with large numbers of servers, services and/or users. Tools like `testparm` and SWAT can be used to assist in certifying correctness. `testparm` validates the syntax and options you have specified for each section of `smb.conf`. If a host name or IP address is supplied as an option, it will check the access rights of the specified host.

```
$ testparm < -s configfilename> <hostname hostIP>
```

SWAT is a system administration tool that provides html forms for each section in smb.conf (Figure 15.2). SWAT can be used to simplify general configuration tasks allowing the system administrator to focus on the section parameter definitions of interest.

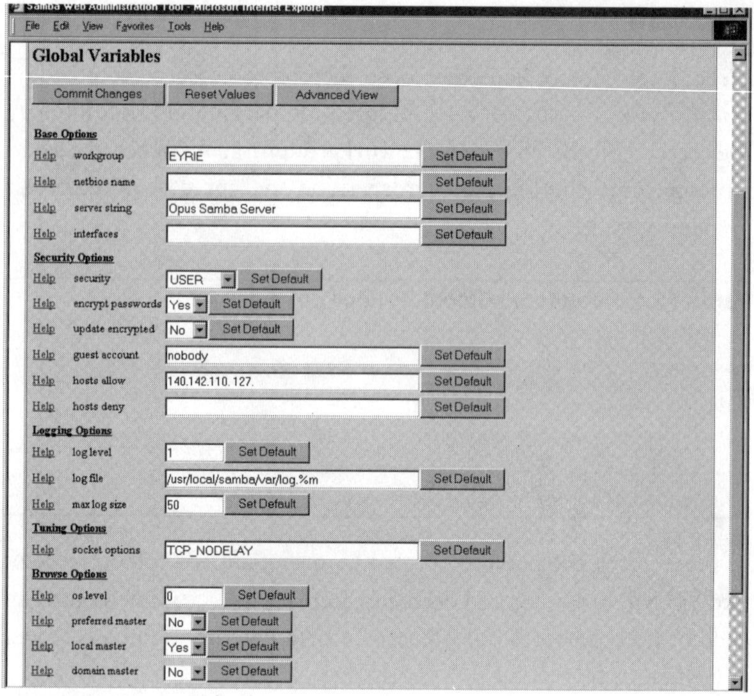

Figure 15.2   *SWAT*

Authentication

There are many things that can go wrong when setting up authentication mechanisms. Here are a few suggestions for ferreting out bugs in the standard Samba authentication schemas.

- Check the `encrypt passwords` parameter for plain-text or NTLM-encrypted password format.
- If they are plain-text passwords, confirm that the UNIX `passwd` file path is correct or that the remote authentication server is identified.
- You may need to fine-tune string guessing permutations to correctly guess uppercased user names and passwords.
- If there are encrypted passwords, then verify that the `smbpasswd` file exists, is populated with users, and is correctly formatted, or that the remote authentication server is identified.

- For Samba domain controllers, check to see that the `netlogin` share has been defined. Validate using `smbclient -U` to test authentication.

Shares

Assuming that authentication problems aren't keeping you from accessing a share, the most likely culprit is access control. Carefully substantiate that you haven't blocked client access due to global `hosts deny` restrictions. Are read-write permissions being applied the way you expect?

To verify general access, use `smbclient` to connect a common share like a home directory defined by the `[homes]` section in `smb.conf` (Example 15.13). Any share will do. Invoke `smbclient` with the share name. If the share requires authentication, you should be prompted for a password. Once the share is authenticated, you should have access to it.

Example 15.13   *Samba Home Share Access*

```
$ smbclient //wizard/deroest
Password:
Domain = [EYRIE] OS = [Unix] Serve r= [Samba 2.0.5a]
Smb: \>
```

Also try connecting the share from a Windows client using the **NET USE** command or **Windows Explorer → Tools → Map** a Network Device (Figure 15.3).

```
C:\NET USE J: \\<server NetBIOS name>\<share name>
```

In the case of printer shares, make sure that you have correctly identified `printcap` printers and that they are marked as `printable`. Next confirm that the `printing os` type is set and that it corresponds to the `print command` and `lpq command` parameters.

If you are providing downloadable Windows 9x printer drivers, verify that the `printer driver name` and `printer driver location` directory are correct and readable. The `printer driver name` is case sensitive and must exactly match the name expected by the Windows driver install procedure. Always print a test page as part of the Windows network printer driver install to make sure features like fonts and colors are working as expected.

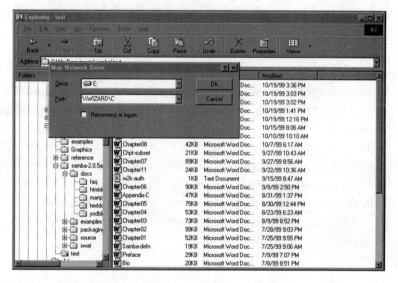

Figure 15.3   *Windows Explorer – map network device*

Use `testprns` to quickly determine whether a given printer name is valid for use. It is a good idea always to specify the `printcap` file as a command argument when testing access. Supply the full path name of the `printcap` file as an argument to limit confusion.

```
$ testprns <printer name> [<printcap-file>]
```

Performance

When it comes to tweaking additional cycles out of Samba, one of the first suggestions is to dedicate one or more computers to the service. This allows you to tune and tailor the operating system to meet Samba's resource demands. It also limits the number of things that go wrong. It is not uncommon in UNIX to have one service severely influence or interrupt another service if they are running on the same hardware.

You might also consider setting up a "cluster" of Samba servers and distributing load across the cluster. Clusters often require the use of hybrid name services that map a service name to multiple IP addresses.

Use OS native performance monitoring tools to gauge the general wellness of the server platform. Again, this will be much easier if Samba is the only service running on the machine. Look for problems indicated by high CPU activity, large amounts of spawned processing, long scheduling queues, large memory usage, and high paging rates.

System sluggishness related to IO can be monitored using the UNIX `iostat` command. Use the `-d` option to display disk IO activity. For each disk, statistics include the number of transfers per second, bytes transferred per second and milliseconds per average seek. Note that not all drive types will report seek times. You can also specify a time interval and count for recording activity snapshots over time.

```
# iostat -d [drive ...] [interval] [count]
```

Take a close look at Samba locking options. For shares that require locking, it is a good idea to make sure that opportunistic locking (oplock) parameters are enabled. `oplocks` allow clients to use aggressive caching and can achieve performance improvements over standard locking by as much as 30%. Also consider disabling **strict locking**. When enabled, **strict locking** directs the server to check lock status on every file access.

The majority of network tuning should be handled at the OS level. Samba does provide a `socket option` parameter for adjusting tcp and socket settings like buffer size and keep alive time (Table 15.5). The tcp_nodelay value is the only one enabled by default. Any value adjustments made with these parameters need to fit corresponding OS level settings.

```
socket option = <value list>

socket option = tcp_nodelay so_reuseaddr
```

Table 15.5   *Samba Socket Option Values*

```
so_keepalive
so_reuseaddr
so_broadcast
tcp_nodelay
iptos_lowdelay
iptos_throughput
so_sndbuf=<integer>
so_rcvbuf=<integer>
so_sndlowat=<integer>
so_rcvlowat=<integer>
```

Logging

It is always nice to have help when debugging a problem. One of the best ways to get help is by setting verbose logging and diagnostic options. You'll need to make tradeoffs between performance hits due to generous logging activity and the problem state. Turn diagnostics up during incident sleuthing and down during normal operation.

Log file and general diagnostic behavior is determined by the `log file`, `max log size`, and `debug level` parameters. Log files normally reside in the `/usr/local/samba/var` directory. By using substitution variables in the log file name, it is possible to generate logs by user, client NetBIOS name, or architecture. By default both `smbd` and `nmbd` generate logs named `log.smb` and `log.nmb`. The `max log size` parameter is used to indicate when a log should be closed out, renamed to `log.old`, and a new log started. Message verbosity is controlled by the **debug level** value. Values range upward from 0. A special value of 100 combined with the `passwd chat debug` setting will record passwords in the log file.

```
log file = /usr/local/samba/var/log.%m
max log size = 10000
debug level = 3
```

Another option is to use the `syslog` and `syslog` only parameters to send Samba messages to the `syslogd` daemon. The `syslog` parameter indicates how Samba debug levels are mapped to corresponding syslog levels. You direct Samba only to log messages via `syslogd`. This might be useful when using `syslogd` to send logs to a common collection site either on the local machine or at a remote log server.

Backups

If you don't have backups then none of the rest of this information is going to do you much good. Every good system administrator knows that system recovery and resumption capability is only as robust as the backup strategy. For a Samba server, this primarily means maintaining backup copies of system configuration files like `smb.conf`, password databases like `smbpasswd`, and critical share data.

You can also use the Samba `smbtar` command to back up and restore remote directory shares (Example 15.14). The target share may be owned by a Windows client or another Samba server. `smbtar` can be incorporated into UNIX shell scripts to automate backup operations using timed batch services like `cron`.

Example 15.14   *smbtar - Dump & Restore*

Incremental Dump

```
Smbtar -s <NetBIOS name> -p <password> -x <Share Name> \
       <device> -I
```

Restore Share

```
Smbtar -s <NetBIOS name> -p <password> -x <Share Name> \
       <device> -r
```

Help

There is always a time in each system administrator's career when outside assistance is required. This is not something we often talk about, but it does happen from time to time. It goes without saying that you've thoroughly perused all the documentation provided in the distribution `samba-<version>/docs` directory and the ancillary text on the Samba web site, **http://samba.org** (Figure 15.4).

When you need that extra configuration tip or just want to commiserate with the rest of the Samba world check the mail lists and news groups listed in Table 15.6.

Figure 15.4   *Samba Web site*

Table 15.6   *Samba Help*

Web Site	
Samba.org	Mirrored Samba Web site

Mail Lists	
samba	The Samba SMB fileserver
samba.digest	Digest form of Samba list
samba.announce	Samba announcements
samba-ntdom	NT domain controller support
samba-vms	Samba for VMS
samba-cvs	Samba CVS commit messages
samba-docs	Discussion about Samba documentation
samba-binaries	Developer discussions about Samba binary distributions

continued on next page

Table 15.6 *continued*

| samba-technical | Developer discussions about Samba internals |
| mirrors | Samba mirror sites |

To subscribe to a list e-mail: **listproc@samba.org** with "subscribe *listname* Your Full Name"* in the message body. For additional information see **http://lists.samba.org/**.

Newsgroups

| comp.protocols.smb | SMB protocol discussions |
| linux.samba | Linux Samba issues |

T-shirts

As a closing note, show your camaraderie with other Samba aficionados by buying and wearing a Samba T-shirt. The price is right. They come in a number of sizes. You can get them on the Samba Web site. As the shirt says, you're *"opening windows to a wider world"*!

Summary

- Work through a problem one subsystem at a time beginning with the lowest common denominator.
- Verify network connectivity using `ifconfig`, `winipcfg`, `netstat`, and `ping`.
- Check Samba daemon operation using `ps`, `netstat`, `smbstatus`, and `smbclient`.
- Test connectivity from Windows clients by using the **NET** command or **Windows Explorer → Tools → Map a Network Drive.**
- Use `nmblookup` to confirm name service operation.
- Windows NBTSTAT can be used to query various SMB information for workgroup or domain systems.
- Verify syntax and options in the Samba configuration files.

```
Startup    /etc/rc<file> or /etc/inetd.conf
Services   /etc/services
Samba      /usr/local/samba/lib/smbconf
Password   /usr/local/samba/private/smbpasswd
```

- Check `smb.conf` options using the `testparm` command or a GUI configuration tool like SWAT.
- Use `smbclient` to check authentication and share access.
- The `testprns` command can be used to validate access to printer shares.
- Use UNIX tools like `iostat` to monitor system performance.
- The Samba `socket option` parameter is provided to tweak tcp options.
- Set up Samba message logging by setting the `log file`, `max log size`, and `debug level` options.
- Direct Samba messages to UNIX `syslogd` daemon using the `syslog` and `syslog only` parameters.
- Maintain a good set of system backups. Use `smbtar` to back up remote client shares.
- Check the Samba Web site and discussion groups for additional help.
- Don't forget about the Samba T-shirts.

GUI Old Samba Tools and Clients

Samba Admin Tools

bbSAT	Windows Samba configuration tool. **http://www.bb-online.de/etc/bbsat/ samba_body.html**
	HP Samba MPE/iX Samba configuration tool. **http://jazz.external.hp.com/src/samba/ bbsat_index.html**
GSMB	GTK interface to smbpasswd management **http://savage.iut-blagnac.fr/projets/ developpement/gsmb/**
smb-mode.el	Emacs smb.conf edit mode **http://users.gtn.net/frasem/smbmode.html**
SMB2WWW	Web view of network neighborhood **http://samba.org/samba/smb2www/ http://www.scintilla.utwente.nl/users/ frank/smb2www/**
smbconftool	Java smb.conf editor **http://www.eatonweb.com/samba/**
smbedit	Win32 smb.conf configuration tool **http://samba.org/samba/smbedit/intro.htm**
SWAT	Samba distribution administration tool **http://samba.org/cgi-bin/swat/**
Webmin	UNIX administration tool with Samba support **http://www.webmin.com/webmin/**

SMB Clients

DAVE	Macintosh SMB client **http://www.thursby.com**
IBM LAN Client	DOS client **http://www.networking.ibm.com/trl/ trlclnt.html**
Microsoft	Windows and DOS clients **http://www.microsoft.com/**

OS/2   OS/2 client

Sharity   UNIX CIFS client
                  http://www.obdev.at/Products/Sharity.html

SMBFS   Linux SMB file system and LAN information
                  http://samba.sernet.de/linux-lan/

VisionFS   SCO SMB client supports mounting of
                  Windows shares under UNIX.
                  http://www.sco.com

B

Sampling of Samba Commands and Utilities

addtosmbpass   is an awk script which automates adding
                                 users to the smbpasswd file.

make_printerdef

```
msprint.inf "printer driver name" >> printers.def
```

make_printerdef   will set up Windows 9x downloadable
                                printer driver based on msprint.inf and
                                msprint2.inf files.

make_smbcodepage

[c|d] *codepage inputfile outputfile*

make_smbcodepage   compiles or decompiles codepage files for
                                use with the internationalization features
                                of Samba 2.0.

nmbd

```
[-D] [-o] [-a] [-H lmhosts file name] [-d debug level] [-l log file base] \
[-n NetBIOS name] [-p port number] [-s configuration file] \
[-i NetBIOS scope] [-h]
```

nmbd   is a server that understands and can reply
                                to NetBIOS over IP name service
                                requests, like those produced by SMBD/
                                CIFS clients such as Windows 95/98,
                                Windows NT, and LAN Manager clients.
                                It also participates in the browsing proto-
                                cols which make up the Windows "net-
                                work neighborhood" view.

nmblookup

```
[-M] [-R] [-S] [-r] [-A] [-h] [-B broadcast address] \
[-U unicast address] [-d debug level] [-s configuration file] \
[-i NetBIOS scope] [-T] name
```

nmblookup   is used to query NetBIOS names and map
                                them to IP addresses in a network using
                                NetBIOS over TCP/IP queries. The
                                options allow the name queries to be
                                directed at a particular IP broadcast area
                                or to a particular machine. All queries are
                                done over UDP.

pwdump   will create an smbpasswd file based on
                             contents of Windows NT registry account
                             information.

smbclient
```
servicename [password] [-s smb.conf] [-B IP addr] \
[-O socket options][-R name resolve order] [-M NetBIOS name] \
[-i scope] [-N] [-n NetBIOS name] [-d debuglevel] [-P] [-p port] \
[-l log file base] [-h] [-I dest IP] [-E] [-U username] \
[-L NetBIOS name] [-t terminal code] [-m max protocol] \
[-W workgroup] [-T<c|x>IXFqgbNan] [-D directory] \
[-c command string]
```

smbclient   is a client that can "talk" to an SMB/CIFS
                             server. It offers an interface similar to that
                             of the FTP program. Operations include
                             things like getting files from the server to
                             the local machine, putting files from the
                             local machine to the server, retrieving direc-
                             tory information from the server, and so on.

smbd
```
[-D] [-a] [-o] [-d debug level] [-l log file] [-p port number] \
[-O socket options] [-s configuration file] [-i scope] [-P] [-h]
```

smbd   is the server daemon that provides file
                             sharing and printing services to Windows
                             clients. The server provides file space and
                             printer services to clients using the SMB
                             (or CIFS) protocol\&. This is compatible
                             with the LAN Manager protocol, and can
                             service LAN Manager clients. These
                             include MSCLIENT 3.0 for DOS,
                             Windows for Workgroups, Windows 95,
                             Windows NT, OS/2, DAVE for
                             Macintosh, and smbfs for Linux.

smbpasswd
```
[-a] [-d] [-e] [-D debug level] [-n] \
[-r remote_machine] [-R name resolve order] [-m] \
[-j DOMAIN] [-U username] [-h] [-s] username
```

| smbpasswd | program has several different functions, depending on whether or not it is run by the root user. When run as a normal user it allows the user to change the password for an SMB session on any machines that store SMB passwords. |

smbmnt

`mount-point [-u uid] [-g gid] [-f file mode] [-d dir mode]`

| smbmnt | is a helper application used by the smbmount (8) program to do the actual mounting. Smbmnt is meant to be installed setuid root so that normal users can mount their smb shares. It checks whether the user has write permissions on the mount point and then mounts the directory. |

smbmount   `mount-point`

| smbmount | is a UNIX mount for normal users. With this program, normal users can mount smb-filesystems, provided that it is suid root. |

smbstatus

`[-b] [-d] [-L] [-p] [-S] [-s configuration file] [-u username]`

| smbstatus | is a very simple program to list the current Samba connections. |

smbtar

`-s server [-p password] [-x service] [-X] [-d directory] [-u user] \`
`[-t tape] [-b blocksize] [-N filename] [-i] [-r] [-l log level] [-v] filenames`

| smbtar | is a very small shell script on top of smbclient which dumps SMB shares directly to tape. |

smbumount   `mount-point`

| smbumount | is a UNIX umount for normal users. With this program, normal users can unmount smb-filesystems, provided that it is suid root. |

swat

```
[-s smb config file] [-a]
```

swat   allows a Samba administrator to configure
                            the complex smb.conf file via a Web
                            browser. In addition, a SWAT configura-
                            tion page has help links to all the config-
                            urable options in the smb.conf file
                            making it easy for an administrator to look
                            up the effects of any change.

tcpdump_smb   will trace and display contents of SMB
                            packets; it is similar to standard tcpdump
                            utility.

testparm

```
[-s] [config file name] [hostname hostIP]
```

testparm   is a very simple test program to check an
                            smbd configuration file for internal cor-
                            rectness. If this program reports no prob-
                            lems, you can use the configuration file
                            with confidence that smbd will successfully
                            load the configuration file.

testprns

```
printername [printcapname]
```

testprns   is a very simple test program to determine
                            whether a given printer name is valid for
                            use in a service to be provided by smbd.

C

Samba 2.0.5a
smb.conf.default

```
# This is the main Samba configuration file. You should read the
# smb.conf(5) manual page in order to understand the options listed
# here. Samba has a huge number of configurable options (perhaps too
# many!) most of which are not shown in this example
#
# Any line which starts with a ; (semi-colon) or a # (hash)
# is a comment and is ignored. In this example we will use a #
# for commentry and a ; for parts of the config file that you
# may wish to enable
#
# NOTE: Whenever you modify this file you should run the command "testparm"
# to check that you have not many any basic syntactic errors.
#
#======================= Global Settings =========================
[global]

# workgroup = NT-Domain-Name or Workgroup-Name, eg: REDHAT4
   workgroup = MYGROUP

# server string is the equivalent of the NT Description field
   server string = Samba Server

# This option is important for security. It allows you to restrict
# connections to machines which are on your local network. The
# following example restricts access to two C class networks and
# the "loopback" interface. For more examples of the syntax see
# the smb.conf man page
;   hosts allow = 192.168.1. 192.168.2. 127.

# If you want to automatically load your printer list rather
# than setting them up individually then you'll need this
   load printers = yes

# you may wish to override the location of the printcap file
;   printcap name = /etc/printcap

# on SystemV system setting printcap name to lpstat should allow
# you to automatically obtain a printer list from the SystemV spool
# system
;   printcap name = lpstat

# It should not be necessary to specify the print system type unless
# it is non-standard. Currently supported print systems include:
# bsd, sysv, plp, lprng, aix, hpux, qnx
```

```
;   printing = bsd


# Uncomment this if you want a guest account, you must add this to /etc/passwd
# otherwise the user "nobody" is used
;  guest account = pcguest


# this tells Samba to use a separate log file for each machine
# that connects
   log file = /usr/local/samba/var/log.%m


# Put a capping on the size of the log files (in Kb).
   max log size = 50


# Security mode. Most people will want user level security. See
# security_level.txt for details.
   security = user
# Use password server option only with security = server
;    password server = <NT-Server-Name>


# You may wish to use password encryption. Please read
# ENCRYPTION.txt, Win95.txt and WinNT.txt in the Samba documentation.
# Do not enable this option unless you have read those documents
;  encrypt passwords = yes


# Using the following line enables you to customise your configuration
# on a per machine basis. The %m gets replaced with the netbios name
# of the machine that is connecting
;    include = /usr/local/samba/lib/smb.conf.%m


# Most people will find that this option gives better performance.
# See speed.txt and the manual pages for details
   socket options = TCP_NODELAY


# Configure Samba to use multiple interfaces
# If you have multiple network interfaces then you must list them
# here. See the man page for details.
;    interfaces = 192.168.12.2/24 192.168.13.2/24


# Browser Control Options:
# set local master to no if you don't want Samba to become a master
# browser on your network. Otherwise the normal election rules apply
;    local master = no


# OS Level determines the precedence of this server in master browser
```

```
# elections. The default value should be reasonable
;   os level = 33


# Domain Master specifies Samba to be the Domain Master Browser. This
# allows Samba to collate browse lists between subnets. Don't use this
# if you already have a Windows NT domain controller doing this job
;   domain master = yes


# Preferred Master causes Samba to force a local browser election on startup
# and gives it a slightly higher chance of winning the election
;   preferred master = yes


# Use only if you have an NT server on your network that has been
# configured at install time to be a primary domain controller.
;   domain controller = <NT-Domain-Controller-SMBName>


# Enable this if you want Samba to be a domain logon server for
# Windows95 workstations.
;   domain logons = yes


# if you enable domain logons then you may want a per-machine or
# per user logon script
# run a specific logon batch file per workstation (machine)
;   logon script = %m.bat
# run a specific logon batch file per username
;   logon script = %U.bat


# Where to store roving profiles (only for Win95 and WinNT)
#        %L substitutes for this servers netbios name, %U is username
#        You must uncomment the [Profiles] share below
;   logon path = \\%L\Profiles\%U


# Windows Internet Name Serving Support Section:
# WINS Support - Tells the NMBD component of Samba to enable it's WINS Server
;   wins support = yes


# WINS Server - Tells the NMBD components of Samba to be a WINS Client
#        Note: Samba can be either a WINS Server, or a WINS Client, but NOT both
;   wins server = w.x.y.z


# WINS Proxy - Tells Samba to answer name resolution queries on
# behalf of a non WINS capable client, for this to work there must be
# at least one   WINS Server on the network. The default is NO.
;   wins proxy = yes
```

```
# DNS Proxy - tells Samba whether or not to try to resolve NetBIOS names
# via DNS nslookups. The built-in default for versions 1.9.17 is yes,
# this has been changed in version 1.9.18 to no.
    dns proxy = no


#========================== Share Definitions ============================
[homes]
    comment = Home Directories
    browseable = no
    writable = yes


# Un-comment the following and create the netlogon directory for Domain Logons
; [netlogon]
;    comment = Network Logon Service
;    path = /usr/local/samba/lib/netlogon
;    guest ok = yes
;    writable = no
;    share modes = no



# Un-comment the following to provide a specific roving profile share
# the default is to use the user's home directory
;[Profiles]
;    path = /usr/local/samba/profiles
;    browseable = no
;    guest ok = yes



# NOTE: If you have a BSD-style print system there is no need to
# specifically define each individual printer
[printers]
    comment = All Printers
    path = /usr/spool/samba
    browseable = no
# Set public = yes to allow user 'guest account' to print
    guest ok = no
    writable = no
    printable = yes


# This one is useful for people to share files
;[tmp]
;    comment = Temporary file space
;    path = /tmp
```

```
;    read only = no
;    public = yes


# A publicly accessible directory, but read only, except for people in
# the "staff" group
;[public]
;    comment = Public Stuff
;    path = /home/samba
;    public = yes
;    writable = yes
;    printable = no
;    write list = @staff


# Other examples.
#
# A private printer, usable only by fred. Spool data will be placed in fred's
# home directory. Note that fred must have write access to the spool directory,
# wherever it is.
;[fredsprn]
;    comment = Fred's Printer
;    valid users = fred
;    path = /homes/fred
;    printer = freds_printer
;    public = no
;    writable = no
;    printable = yes


# A private directory, usable only by fred. Note that fred requires write
# access to the directory.
;[fredsdir]
;    comment = Fred's Service
;    path = /usr/somewhere/private
;    valid users = fred
;    public = no
;    writable = yes
;    printable = no


# a service which has a different directory for each machine that connects
# this allows you to tailor configurations to incoming machines. You could
# also use the %U option to tailor it by user name.
# The %m gets replaced with the machine name that is connecting.
;[pchome]
;    comment = PC Directories
;    path = /usr/pc/%m
```

```
;   public = no
;   writable = yes


# A publicly accessible directory, read/write to all users. Note that all files
# created in the directory by users will be owned by the default user, so
# any user with access can delete any other user's files. Obviously this
# directory must be writable by the default user. Another user could of course
# be specified, in which case all files would be owned by that user instead.
;[public]
;     path = /usr/somewhere/else/public
;     public = yes
;     only guest = yes
;     writable = yes
;     printable = no


# The following two entries demonstrate how to share a directory so that two
# users can place files there that will be owned by the specific users. In this
# setup, the directory should be writable by both users and should have the
# sticky bit set on it to prevent abuse. Obviously this could be extended to
# as many users as required.
;[myshare]
;     comment = Mary's and Fred's stuff
;     path = /usr/somewhere/shared
;     valid users = mary fred
;     public = no
;     writable = yes
;     printable = no
;     create mask = 0765
```

Bibliography

Jeremy Alison, "Doing the NIS/NT Samba," *Linux World*, October 1998.

John D. Blair, "Samba: Integrating UNIX and Windows," Specialized Systems Consultants, Inc., 1998.

Jim Boyce Christa Anderson, Axel Larson, et al., "Windows NT Workstation 4.0 Advanced Technical Reference," Indianapolis, IN: Que Corporation, 1996.

Eric Car, "The New King of the Hill," Sm@rt Reseller Online, *ZDNet*, Ziff-Davis, Inc., April 5, 1999.

Gerald Carter, "Administering Windows NT Domains Using a non-Windows NT PDC," Proceedings of the 2nd Large Installation System Administration of Windows NT Conference, USENIX SAGE, July 14-17, 1999.

Pankaj Chowdhry, "Samba up-tempo performer," *ZDNet*, Ziff-Davis, Inc., March 14, 1999.

Paul Leach and Dan Perry, "Standardizing Internet File Systems with CIFS." Microsoft Internet Developer, November 1996.

Joseph Moran and Jacquelyn Gavron, "Securing Files with NT," *Windows Sources*, ZD Press, July 1998 "Microsoft WindowsNT ResourceKit," Microsoft Press, 1996.

"Protocols for X/Open PC Interworking: SMB, Version 2," The Open Group, X/Open Document Number: C209, 1992.

RFC 1001 "Protocol Standard for a NetBIOS Service on a TCP/UDP Transport: Concepts and Methods," Network Working Group, Internet Engineering Task Force, March 1987.

RFC 1002 "Protocol Standard for a NetBIOS Service on a TCP/UDP Transport: Detailed Specification," Network Working Group, Internet Engineering Task Force, March 1987.

W. Richard Stevens, *UNIX Network Programming*, Prentice-Hall, Inc., Englewood Cliffs, NJ, 1990.

Steven B. Thomas, *Windows NT: Heterogeneous Networking*, Indianapolis, IN: Macmillan Technical Publishing, 1999.

Thursby Software, "CIFS World," http://www.thursby.com/cifs/, Thursby Software Systems, Inc, 5840 W. Interstate 20, Arlington, Texas 76017.

Steven J. Vaughan-Nichols and Eric Car, "Samba 2.0: A License to Kill NT?," Sm@rt Reseller Online, *ZDNet*, Ziff-Davis, Inc., March 22, 1999.

G. Robert Williams and Ellen Beck Gardner, *Windows NT & UNIX*, Reading, MA: Addison-Westley, Longman, Inc., 1998.

Index

Note: Boldface numbers indicate illustrations.

293